Vintage Children's Fabric

Kay Hanauer

4880 Lower Valley Road   Atglen, Pennsylvania   19310

Acknowledgments

A special thanks to Cindy, who accompanies me in my travels and found many of these items; to Linda for great advice and editing skills; and to my grandchildren for showing me how to transfer these pictures.

Thanks also to Rita Davis, who gave her valuable time to offer her expert opinion on fabric age; to Brian Dewitt, whose photography skills covered most of the wrinkles, and finally to Bryan and the other guys with Budget PC for soothing my panic and repairing my computer glitches.

Other Schiffer Books on Related Subjects:
Japanese Children's Fabric, 0-7643-1967-1, $34.95
Vintage Feed Sacks, 0-7643-2611-2, $29.95
The Well-Dressed Child: Children's Clothing 1820s-1950s, 0-7643-0858-0, $39.95

Cover and book designed by: Bruce Waters
Type set in Futura XBlk BT and Humanst521 BT

ISBN: 978-0-7643-3855-7
Printed in China

Schiffer Books are available at special discounts for bulk purchases for sales promotions or premiums. Special editions, including personalized covers, corporate imprints, and excerpts can be created in large quantities for special needs. For more information contact the publisher:

Published by Schiffer Publishing Ltd.
4880 Lower Valley Road
Atglen, PA 19310
Phone: (610) 593-1777; Fax: (610) 593-2002
E-mail: Info@schifferbooks.com

For the largest selection of fine reference books on this and related subjects, please visit our website at:
www.schifferbooks.com
We are always looking for people to write books on new and related subjects. If you have an idea for a book, please contact us at
proposals@schifferbooks.com

This book may be purchased from the publisher.
Include $5.00 for shipping.
Please try your bookstore first.
You may write for a free catalog.

In Europe, Schiffer books are distributed by
Bushwood Books
6 Marksbury Ave.
Kew Gardens
Surrey TW9 4JF England
Phone: 44 (0) 20 8392 8585; Fax: 44 (0) 20 8392 9876
E-mail: info@bushwoodbooks.co.uk
Website: www.bushwoodbooks.co.uk

Contents

Introduction

Oh, the fun of collecting! My first experience (pencils) was in elementary school. They were less than a nickel, and I loved to organize them in rainbow order. Then it was bead collecting — a necklace for each outfit was a must! Through the years, I've collected buttons, old lace, children's sewing machines, postage stamps, quilt/craft books (over 650 at last count), and vintage cigar bands (13,000 different ones). Much of the excitement came from visiting antique shops or shows in surrounding states — getting up early each Saturday, traveling to new places, and happily reviewing purchases on the long ride home. During these various obsessions, I was always searching for quilt fabric.

Although the new fabrics are amazingly beautiful, somehow I was drawn to the vintage fabrics from my childhood. As several in my family are quilters, I was fortunate to have advice from an excellent teacher, my mom, whose perfect, tiny stitches I could never emulate. Her fabric was used in my first quilt, begun while expecting my first child, Cindy. I found the small sack of unfinished pieces several years ago and completed the quilt top for her 40th birthday.

Lately my focus has been vintage children's fabric, with a special love of those from the early part of the twentieth century. If fabric width was available, I purchased only narrow width fabric produced before middle 1960s, generally 36" wide. However, many finds were from vintage children's clothing, aprons, or quilts. There are a variety of fabrics — feed sacks, flannel, seersucker, cotton, and one silk. Although my original scans are actual size, some of the prints are so tiny they were enlarged for the book. To keep track of this growing collection, they were organized by subject. While I'm no authority on the subject, I feel the fabrics

included in this book are from this early period. I hope you enjoy them as much as I do.

This journey started because I could not bear using my wonderful vintage fabrics in a quilt. I thought that if I scanned the fabric into the computer, I'd always have the design. Maybe I could even print it to see how it looks. Where should I begin? I enjoyed the delicate red and blue designs from the 1880s and 1890s; so many different patterns with such few colors. There were also the beautiful pastel fabrics from the 20s and 30s with such varieties of color and design.

Then I found some darling pieces of fabric in my grandmother's quilt top. How wonderful it would be to have this intricate fabric. They were turquoise hexagons of Mary and her lambs. I carefully taped the pieces together, matching as much of the design as possible, and scanned them into my computer. Experimenting with a never-used program purchased several years ago, I erased the overlaps; found the design repeats, and was able to make a sizeable swatch of the fabric.

Searching through my boxes of vintage fabric was a hoot! Each child's fabric discovered was scanned and cloned into a swatch as large as possible. Of course, never satisfied, the search continued at antique shows and shops in surrounding areas. Then I discovered eBay and Etsy. Well, need I say more?

As my collection grew, I wanted to share them with other people who also love vintage designs. Unfortunately, I have no knowledge of the fabric designers, the textile mills that produced the fabric, or the retail stores that sold them. I hope the readers will just use this book to enjoy the sweet children's fabric from earlier times.

Memories of Childhood

These first few fabrics bring back memories of childhood. Mother had dish towels embroidered with the various daily tasks. Each towel had one day of the week with the task for that day — she always washed on Monday and ironed on Tuesday. My sisters and I grudgingly shared in those tasks with her. I haven't yet found fabric depicting Thursday (Going to the Market) or Sunday (Church or Day of Rest).

Monday – washing.

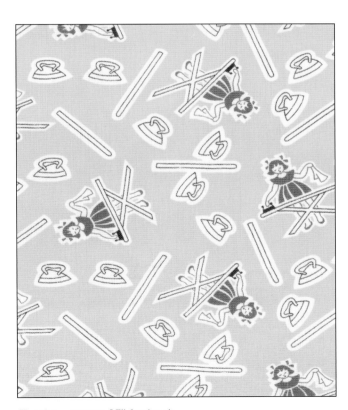

Tuesday – ironing; 37" feed sack.

Wednesday – mending.

Wednesday – mending.

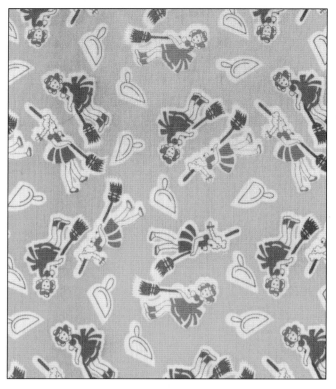

Friday – cleaning.

Saturday – baking; possibly early feed sack, as it is only 24" wide.

Housework, one in orange and the other in red. These are 38" feed sacks.

Chapter One
School and Nursery Rhymes

Children's clothing made with the alphabet fabrics were probably used to encourage little ones to learn. It was interesting that designers not only used A, B, C, and D, but also produced fabrics with other parts of the alphabet.

The nursery rhyme fabrics are some of my favorites, including "This Little Piggy Went to the Market" and "Peter, Peter, Pumpkin Eater." Mr. McGregor is certainly puzzled in Peter Rabbit's

fabric, but my favorite of this group is the red fabric of "Mary Had A Little Lamb." As I mentioned in my Introduction, this design was the first one that I tried copying. It is quite intricate with nine different Mary designs. I was able to complete a swatch in turquoise and later, to my delight, found the red fabric with a complete design.

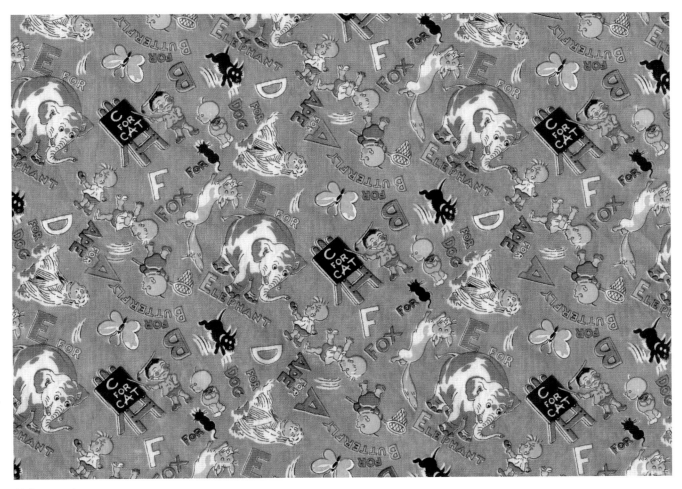

Alpha animals.

ABC play, 35" loosely woven cotton.

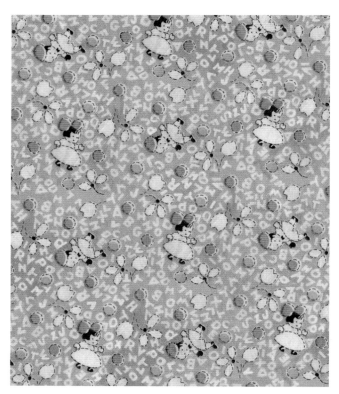

A-B-C ...

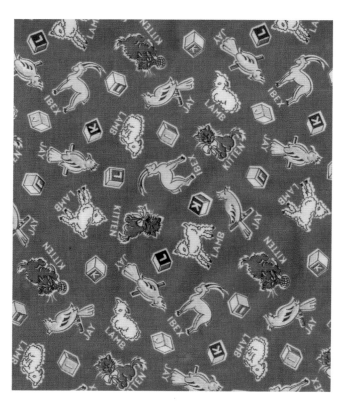

... I-J-K-L ...

... M-N-O-P ...

1-2-3-4-5. This unusual fabric is from a 1920s doll dress. This is the only fabric I've seen with a number design.

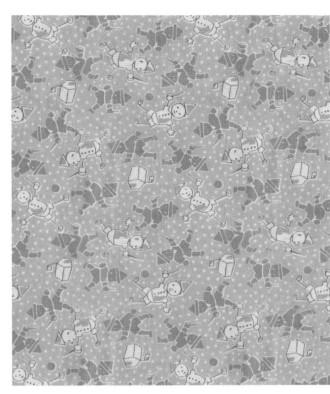

School days.

Studies, percale quality.

Spelling class.

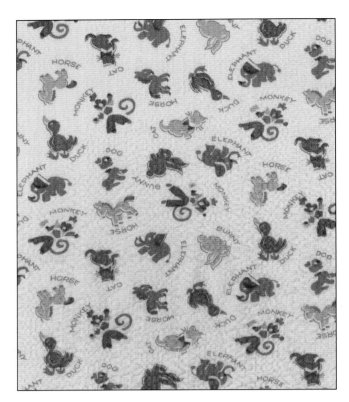

Spelling exercise 1, 30" seersucker.

Spelling exercise 2, 37.5" feed sack. This features the same design as the previous seersucker, but is 25% larger.

ABC lessons, 36" lightweight cotton.

Benny Bunny, Dicky Duck, 37" feed sack.

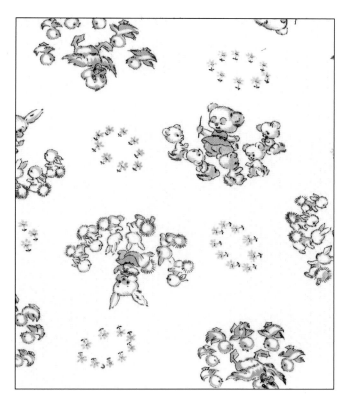

Storytime, 36" seersucker.

Noah's story.

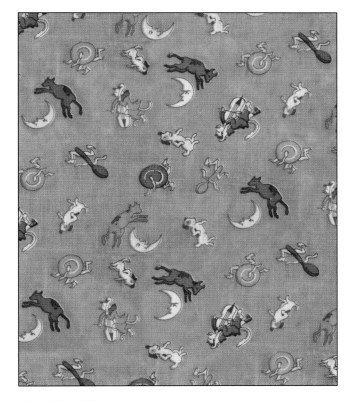

Hey diddle diddle.

The Cat and the Fiddle, 30" seersucker with varied width blisters.

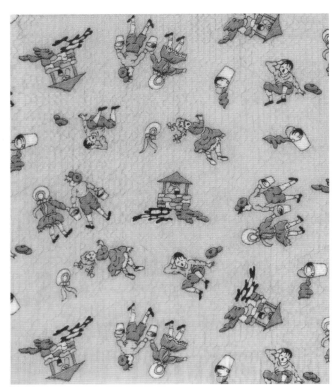

Seersucker from a vintage doll dress. Jack and Jill went up the hill…

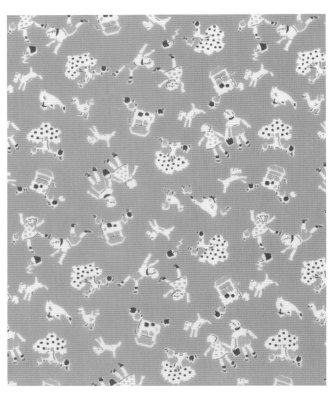

… To fetch a pail of water, 35" percale quality.

Humpty Dumpty, 34.5" tightly woven cotton.

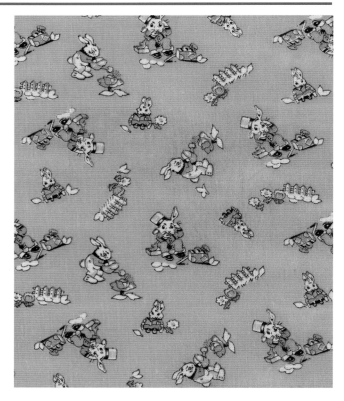

Peter Rabbit. This exceptional fabric was from a child's apron.

Little boy blue, 30.5" seersucker.

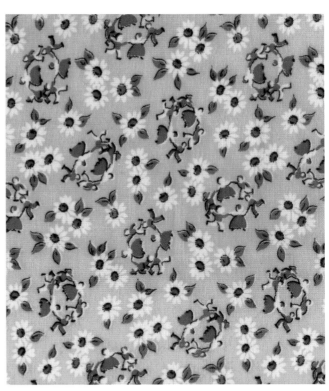

Ring around the Rosie, feed sack fabric

This Little Piggy Went to the Market, 34" percale quality fabric. I had looked at this image many times before finally recognizing the theme.

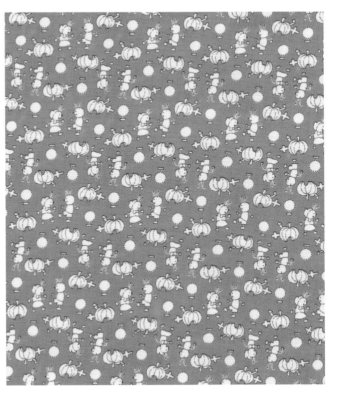

Peter, Peter, Pumpkin Eater. This is a tiny piece of fabric is from a vintage quilt block. It was in my possession for a year before I realized its nursery rhyme subject.

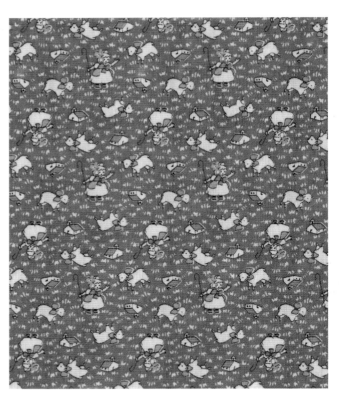

This percale quality fabric is my favorite from the nursery rhyme themed fabrics I have. Mary Had a Little Lamb...

... It followed her to school one day ...

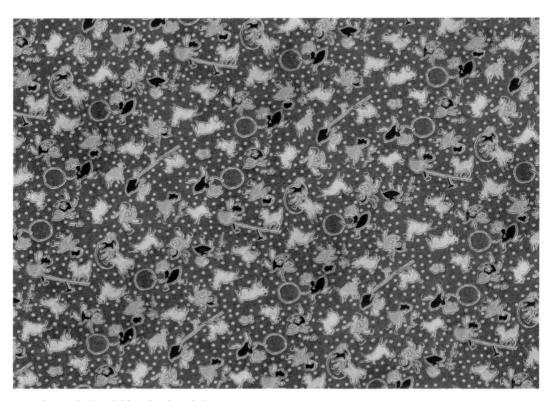

... and it made the children laugh and play.

Mary's lambs.

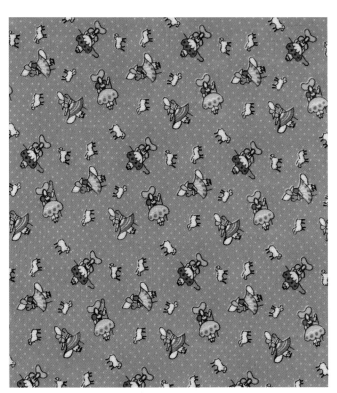

Mary's lambs on green, 37.5" feed sack.

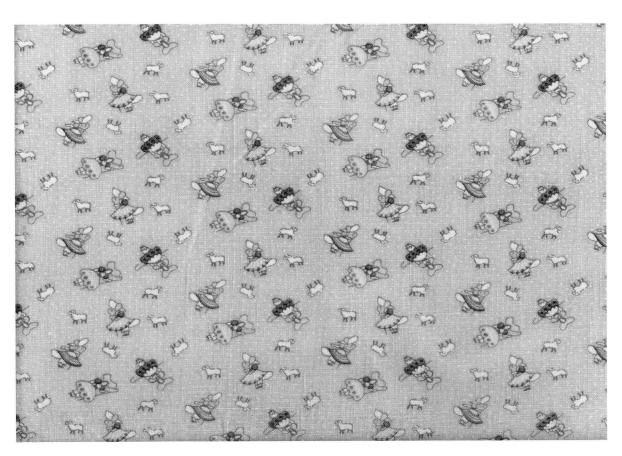

Mary's lambs on pink, 37.5" feed sack.

Nursery Rhymes. This is a 25" wide cotton fabric with a woven stripe similar to dimity.

Nursery rhymes, 36" percale.

Nursery rhymes, 36" percale.

Raggedy Ann and Andy, 35" cotton.

Nursery Rhymes, yellow and white fabric.

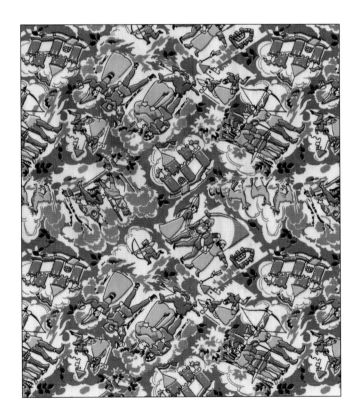

Robin Hood, feed sack fabric.

Robin Hood calls. This is an old-fashioned diaper.

School and Nursery Rhymes

Doctor, Lawyer, Indian chief… This fabric might fit the rhyme, "Rich Man, Poor Man, Beggar Man, Thief." There seems to be a few extra characters, but then the rhyme has many versions.

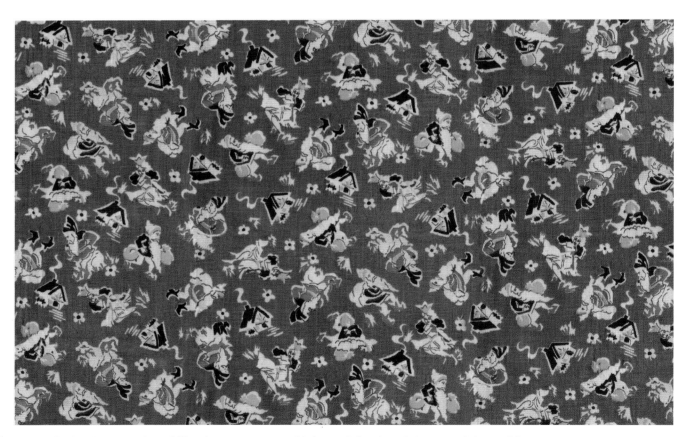

Bags of Gold… A nursery rhyme? This shows two crowned ladies with four bearded men, each having full bags. The bags of one character are gold. There just has to be a story there, somewhere!

Chapter Two
Kids and Parties

Fabrics with small images of children seem to be some of the most highly prized by collectors, perhaps because these sweet, innocent images remind us of our little ones in earlier years.

As I went through the process of collecting and putting the images together for this book, it was interesting to me that the same image was used in different sizes. Designers not only changed the image sizes, but they also used different fabrics.

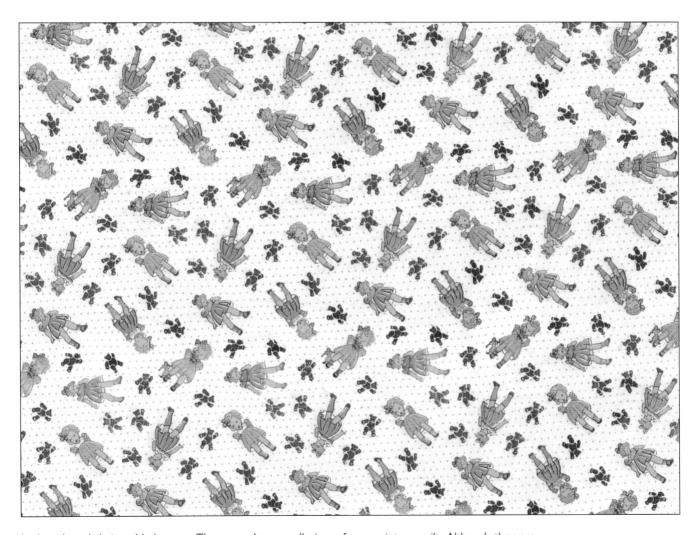

Little girls and their teddy bears... These are three small pieces from a vintage quilt. Although they are somewhat discolored, I wanted to include them here because I haven't seen them anywhere else

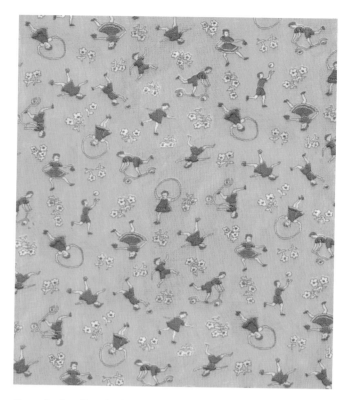

Drop the handkerchief and jump rope.

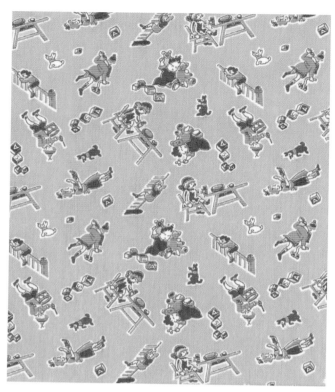

Sliding down the banister and playing with dolly, 36" percale.

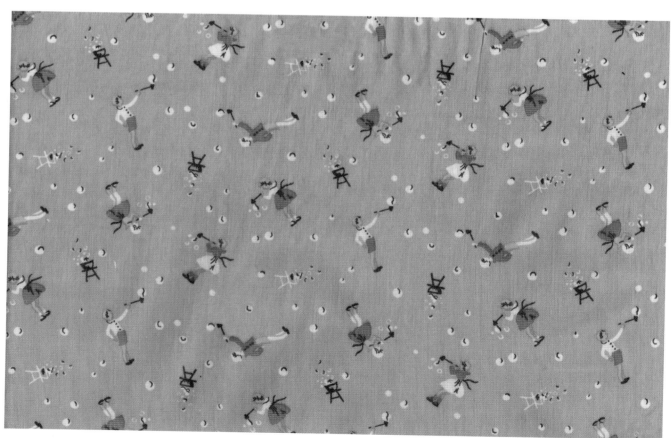

Blowing bubbles.

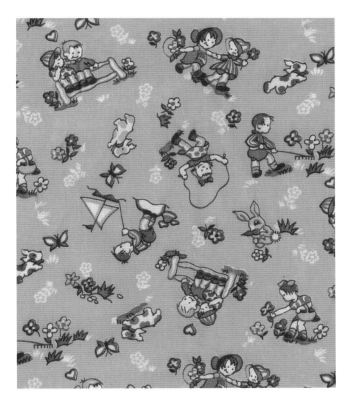

First love… These were oddly shaped fabric scraps, but when cloned them together I found a complete design.

He loves me, he loves me not; 35" polished cotton.

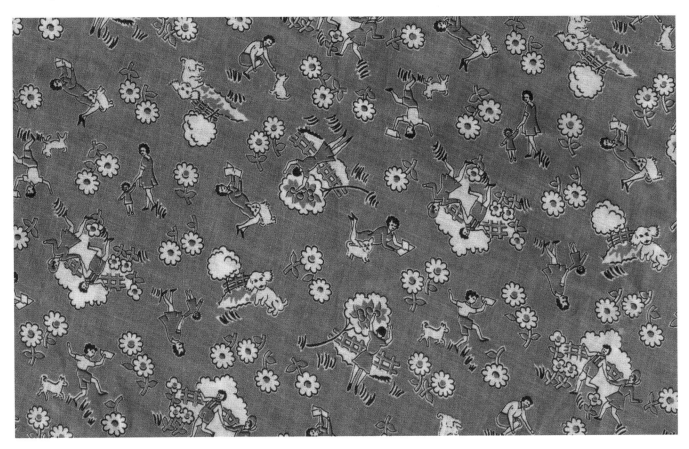

Puppy love.

Garden help.

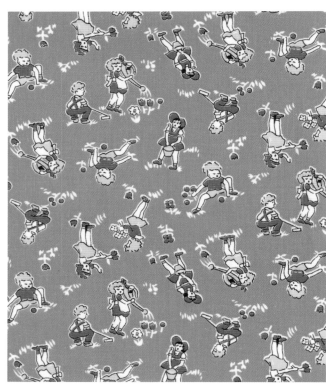

Garden duties, percale quality.

Super heroes, 36" seersucker. This one makes me chuckle. We listened to some of those characters (Superman, Batman, Green Hornet, and the Shadow) on Saturday morning radio as we cleaned the house.

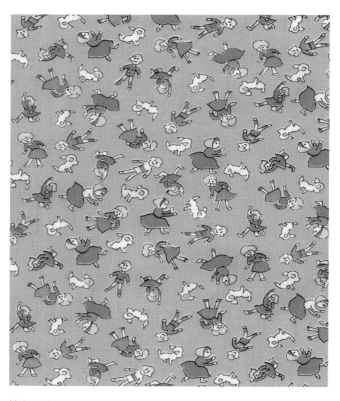

Kids and pups.

 Kids and Parties

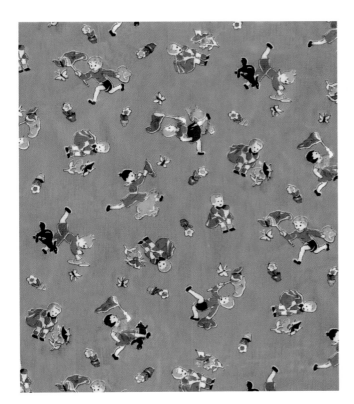

Catching butterflies.

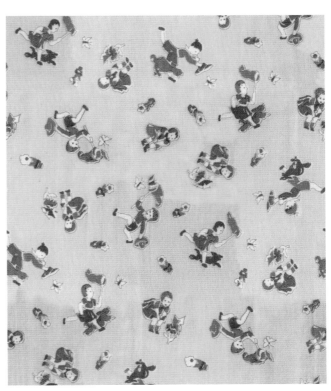

Catching butterflies. This design is smaller in scale than the previous fabric.

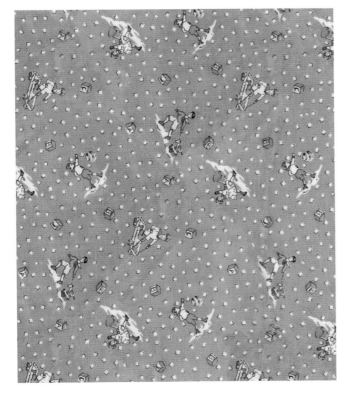

Children at play, in blue and pink.

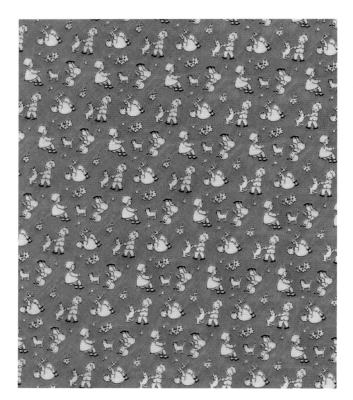

Playful pets.

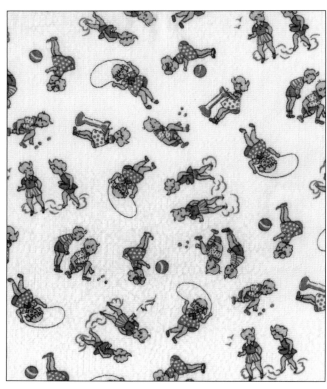

So thirsty, 31" seersucker.

My ponies.

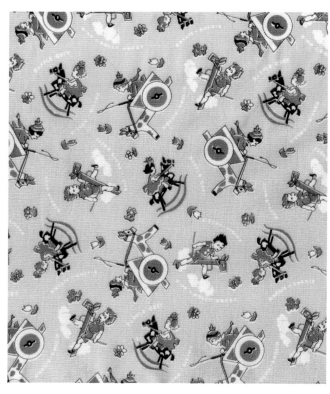

Ride a hobby horse… This fabric appears to have faint messages between the images that say "Ride a hobby horse," "Dapple Gray," and "Dobbie Dobbin."

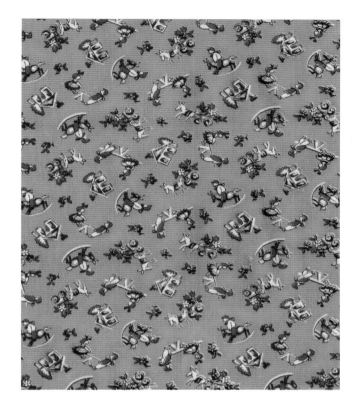

Rocking ride, in red and yellow.

Bath play.

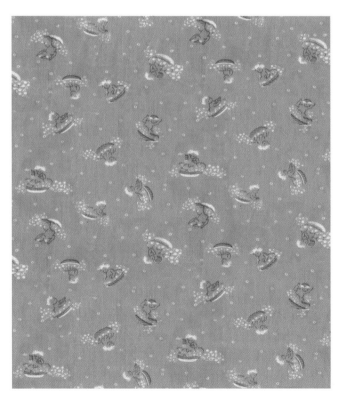

Bathing baby.

Seesaw, yum yum, and pretty.

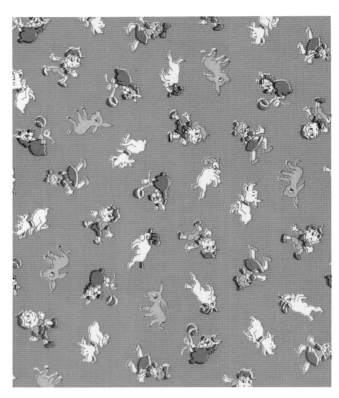

Kids and Billy goat gruff, percale quality.

Playtime, 35" cotton.

Sailing ships… This is probably one of the older fabrics and was a 3" by 6" piece from a vintage quilt block.

 Kids and Parties

Frames, one on blue and the other red; 25" feed sacks.

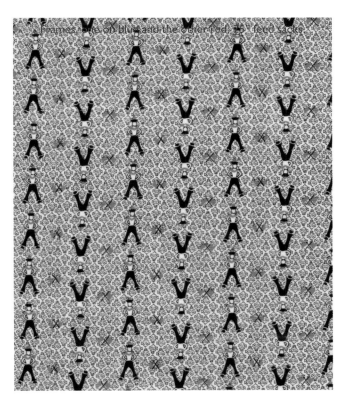

Frames, one on blue and the other red, 25" feed sacks.

Sailors and flags.

Seashore fun, 30" seersucker.

Kids and Parties

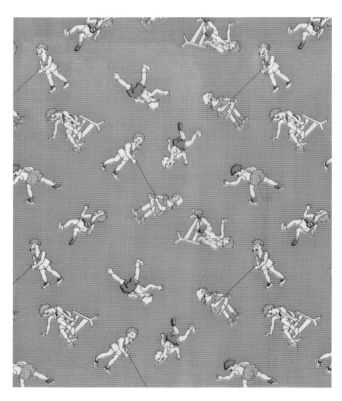

Seashore play… The tiny black dot in this fabric is a fish's eye.

Tug of war, hurdles, and track.

Be careful on those steps! These feed sacks are 39" x 46" and 36", respectively, while the standing boy is approximately 2.75" and 2.25", respectively.

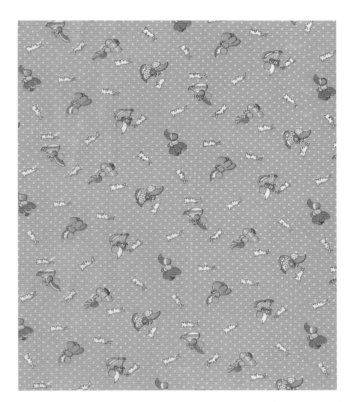
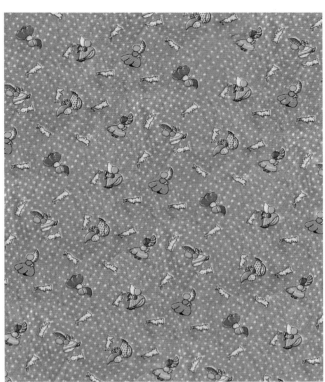

Sunbonnet girls, in red and blue.

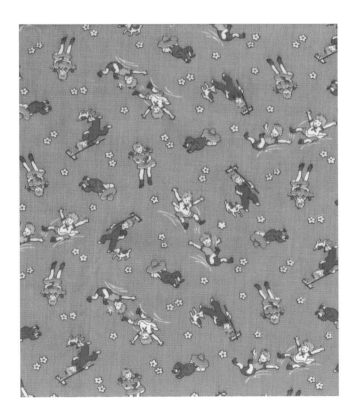
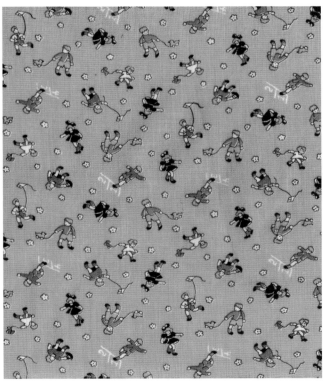

Seat sliding, 35" cotton with slight sheen. Background color is "that vintage green."

Kite flying and hopscotch.

Polo.

Teaching Wiggles… Yes, I had a faithful friend named Wiggles. He knew all my secrets and lived to the ripe old age of fifteen.

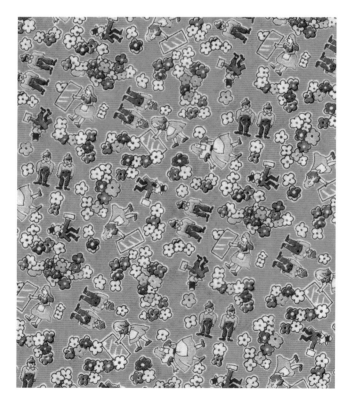

The terrible twins… This image in this fabric is puzzling: Is the girl opening a door? Is the character handing her mail? Or did the terrible twins play a trick? I couldn't figure it out. Can you?

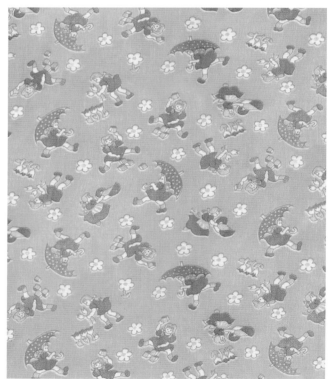

Busy day.

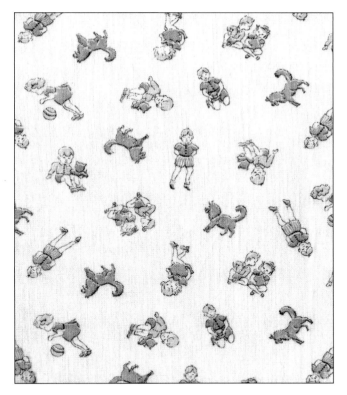

Just hanging around, 37" feed sack.

Paddle play, 35" flannel.

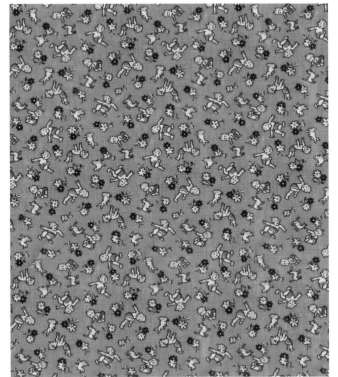

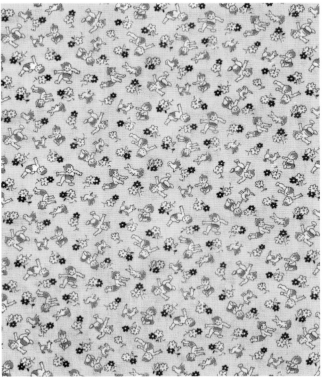

Tumblers, in blue and yellow.

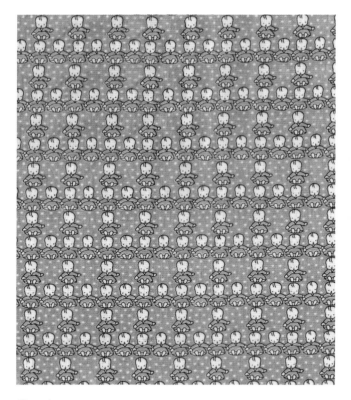

Cherubs.

Flowers for Mama.

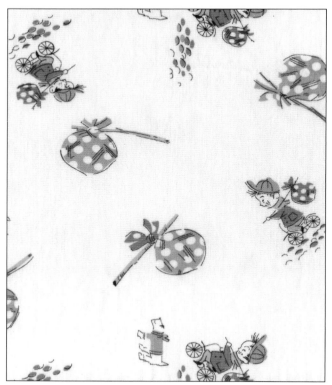

Hobo, in green and blue.

Flower girl.

Senor and senorita, 36" cotton.

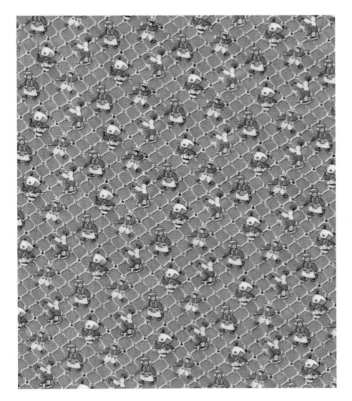

Wooden shoes.

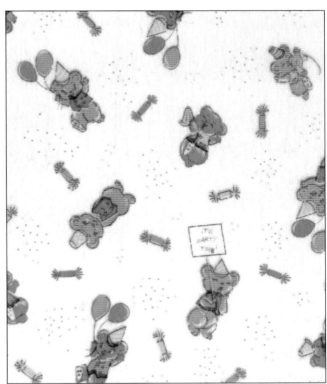

It's a party! Fabric is 35" light weight flannel.

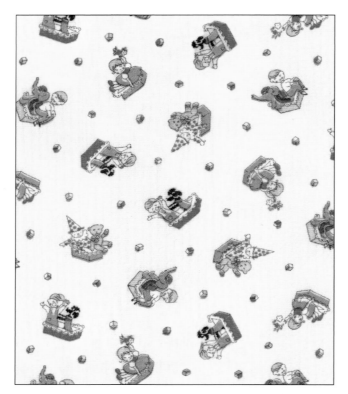

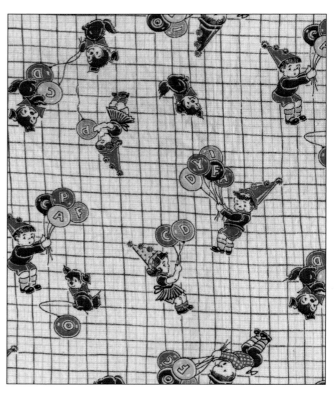

Surprise package. This fabric is from a doll's dress. The design shows children playing in boxes. What better toy is there?

Party balloons, 36" feed sack.

Birthday gifts.

Chapter Three
Leisure and Play

There was such excitement when the circus came to town! These themes were very popular in earlier times, especially before television. Elephants, tigers, clowns, and circus rides and acts are all depicted in the following fabrics.

Dancing is a universal activity and all cultures honor it. We seem to have special interest in costumes from abroad, as indicated by the many folk dancers fabric. A variety of sports are also represented: skiing, soccer, gymnastics, baseball, skating, bowling, basketball, and football.

One fabric seems to reflect a national or international contest, for it includes planes and a foreign village, and the many toy images were sure to please the children.

Circus band. I just love these images… they are bound to make any child smile.

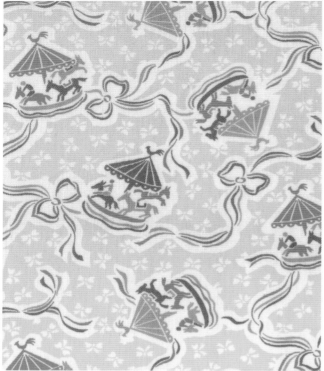

Carousel.

Circus folks.

Elephant slide. I see a similarity in the elephant in this image and the "Alpha Animals" image from Chapter One. I wonder if they were by the same designer.

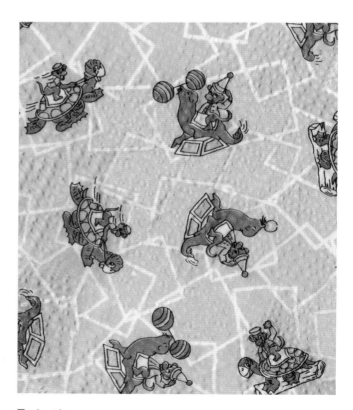

Turtle ride.

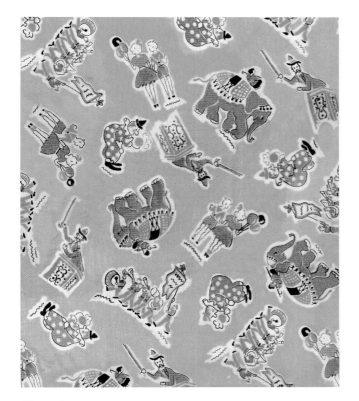

Circus show.

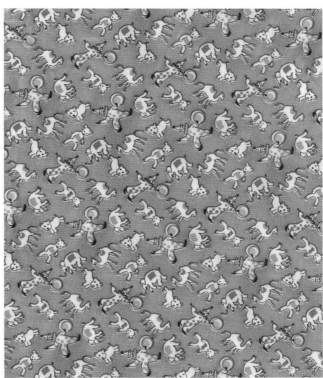

Circus time.

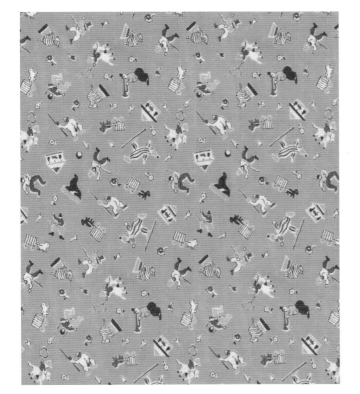

Tigers, seals, and clowns.

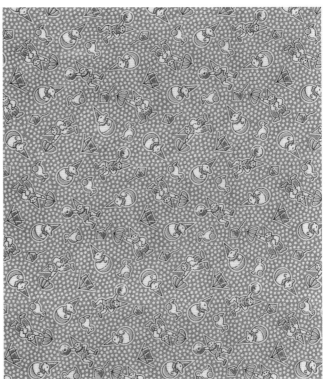

Strongman.

Leisure and Play

Circus day.

Circus acts.

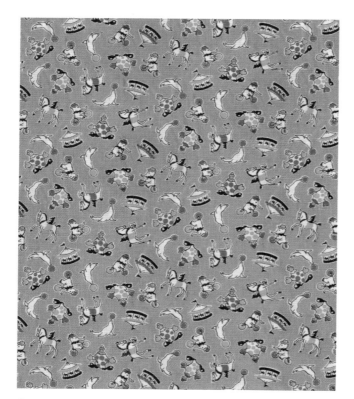

Circus acts.

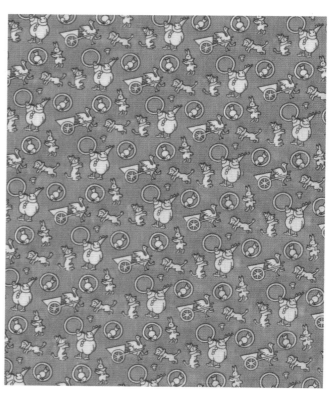

Doggy tricks.

Leisure and Play

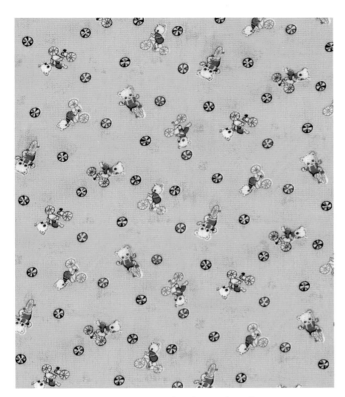

Doggy acrobat... Can you see the daring doggy?
He surely had to practice that trick!

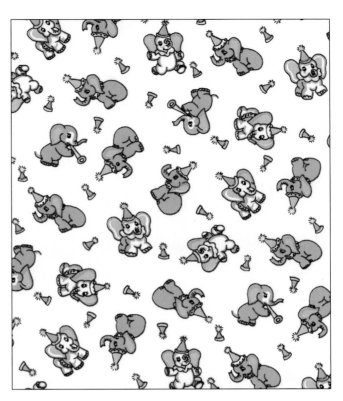

Elephant band.

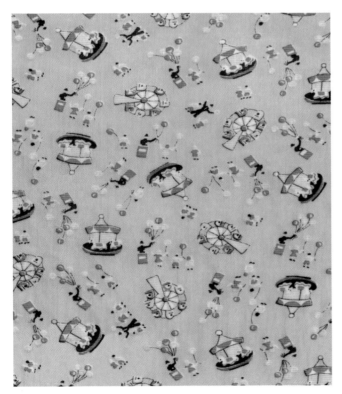

Circus rides.

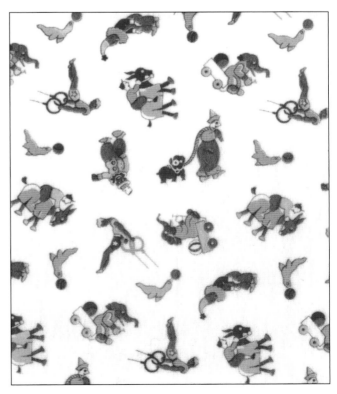

Circus fun, 36" flannel.

Leisure and Play

Three-ring show, 30" very fine seersucker.

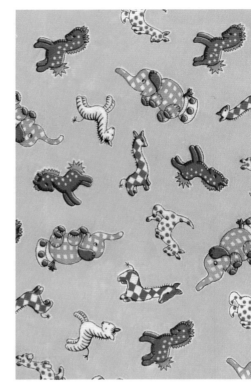

Checks and dots.

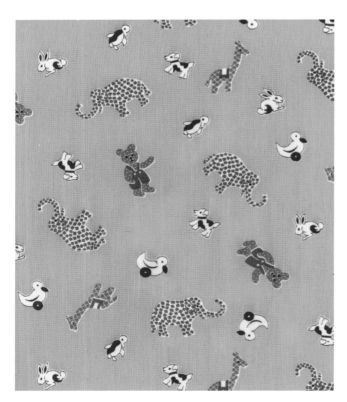

Dots and checks.

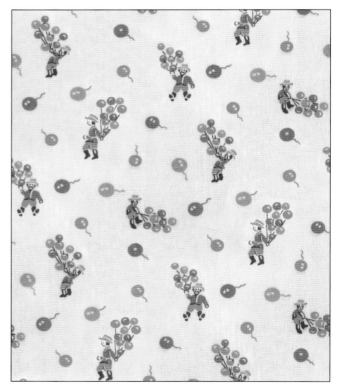

Balloon man.

Leisure and Play

All-day circus, feed sacks, white fabric. One has a black and red pattern
theme and the other a blue and red theme.

Pandas and clowns, 35" percale quality, in red and white.

Leisure and Play

Balloons and bears, 36" medium weight flannel.

Balloons, bears, and bunnies, 37" tightly woven cotton.

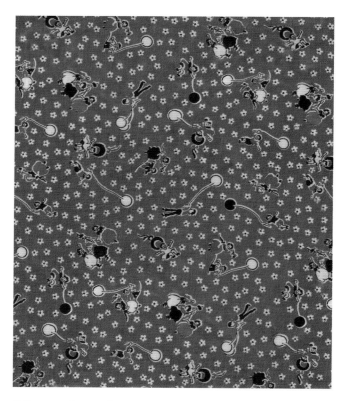

Balloons and maypole.

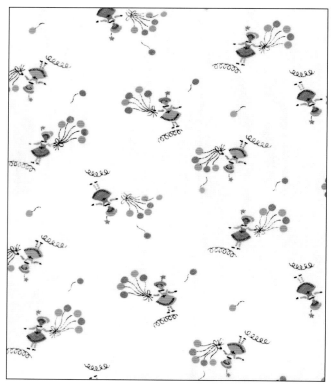

Blue and pink balloons.

Leisure and Play

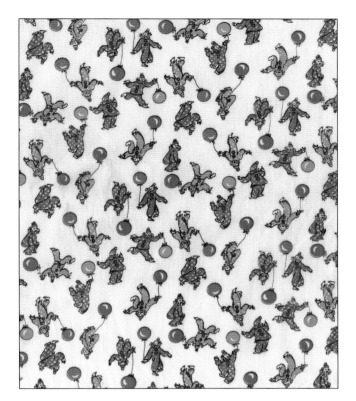
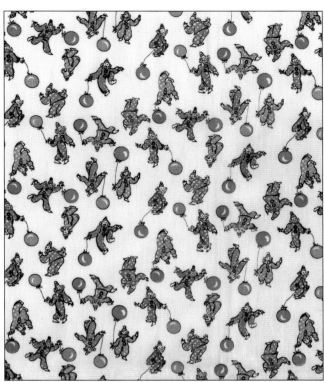

Clowns and balloons. Though the fabrics are similar — 36" tightly woven cotton — again this is another instance where the designs are the same but characters have been made a different size.

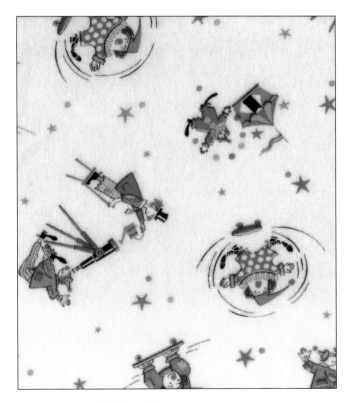

Circus clowning, 36" flannel.

Clowns and ladders.

Leisure and Play

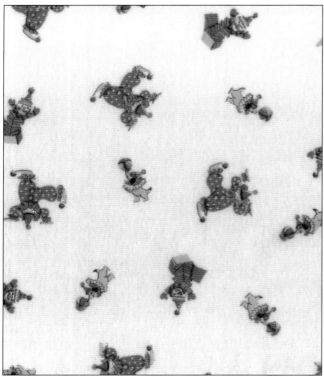

Clowns and jack-in-the-box, 34" flannel.

Tumblers, 35" flannel.

Clowns in green face, 36" feed sack.

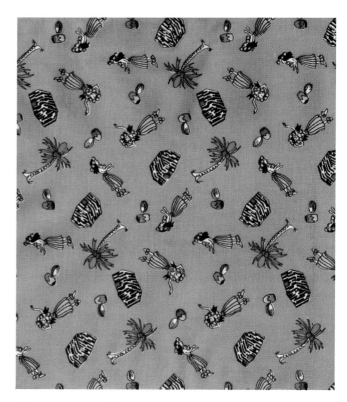

Hawaiian dancer, 36" tightly woven cotton.

Monkey business.

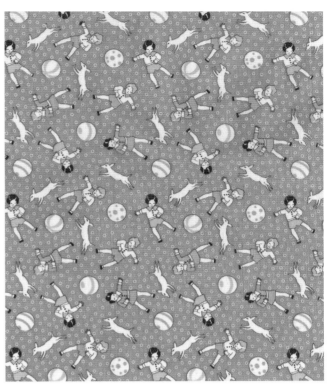

Dancing the samba.

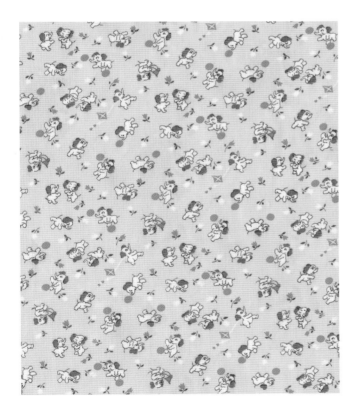

Red-eared elephant.

One-monkey circus, feed sack. This character is not only the circus band, but also the acrobats as well. I guess he's back in his cage, too, because he's eating a banana while hanging from the tree.

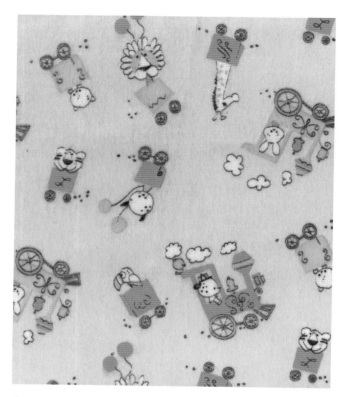

Circus choo-choo, 35" flannel.

Ballerinas, 36" tightly woven cotton.

Ballerinas and ballet slippers.

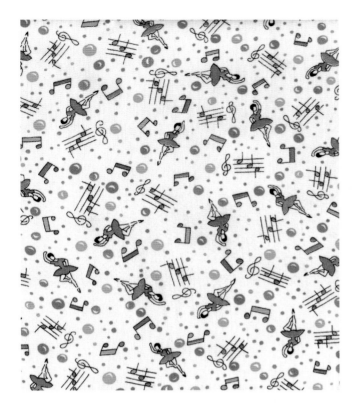

Ballerina music. This fabric was from an apron.

Ballerina dance.

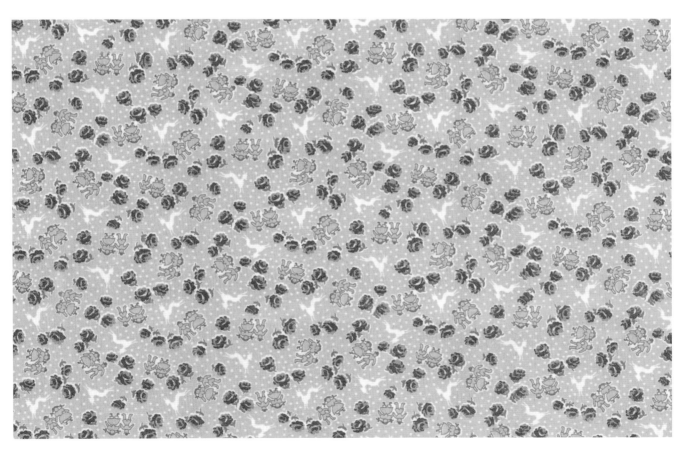

Folk costumes and roses.

Folk costumes, 36" cotton.

Folk dancers, black fabric, 35" cotton.

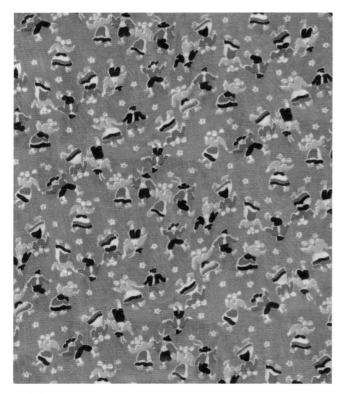

Folk dancers, green fabric.

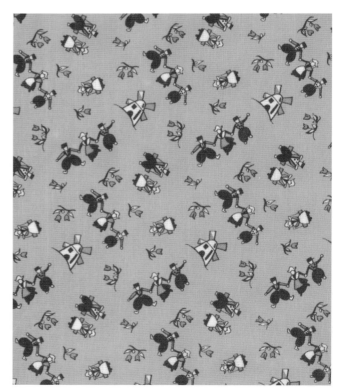

Folk dancers, pink fabric.

Leisure and Play

Folk dancers, red fabric.

Folk dancers, yellow fabric.

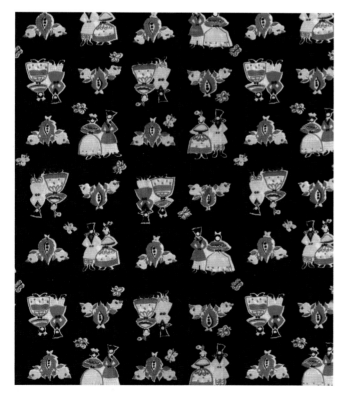

Folk dancers.

Gypsy dancers.

Leisure and Play

Barn dance, feed sacks.

Spanish dancers, 36" feed sacks.

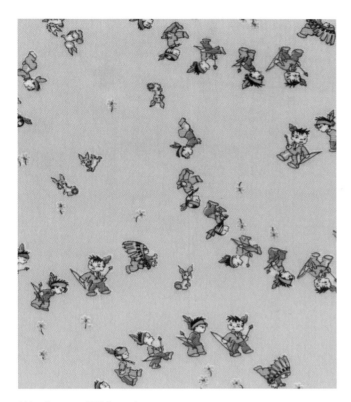

War dancers, 35" flannel.

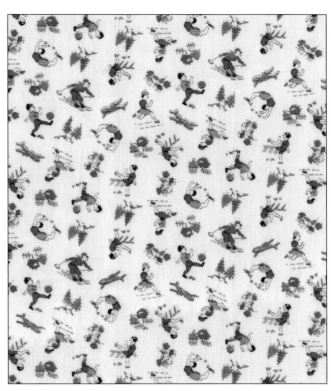

Training exercises.

Baseball. I purchased this fabric around the year 1960.

Skating fun. This fabric is from a pair of child's pajamas.

Sports equipment, 34.5" cotton.

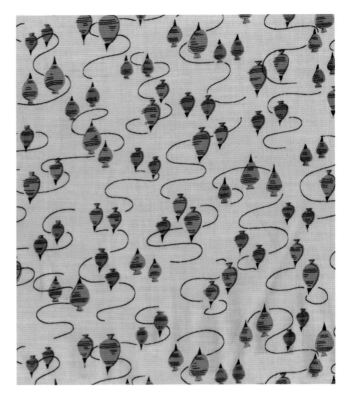

Tops.

Toys for pulling.

Now put your toys away…

Leisure and Play

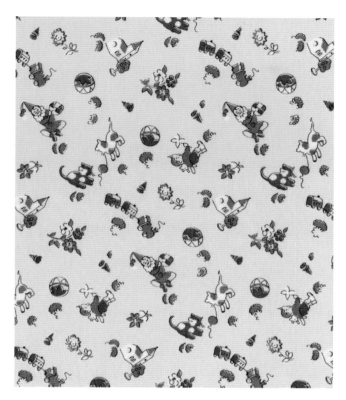

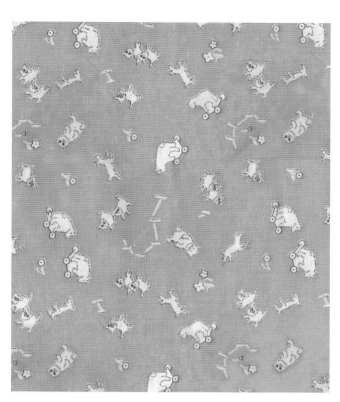

... You may play after your nap. Vendor purchased this 29" width fabric in Germany.

Toys resting.

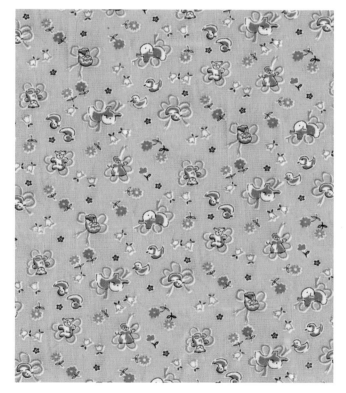

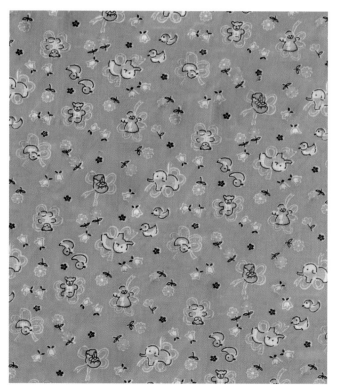

Toys with bows, pink and green.

Leisure and Play

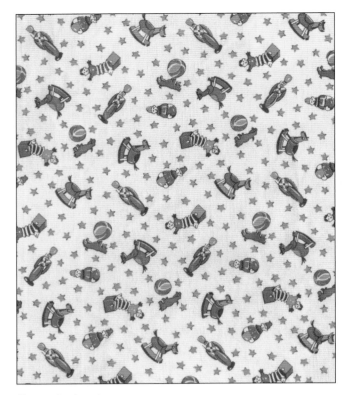

Toys and roly poly.

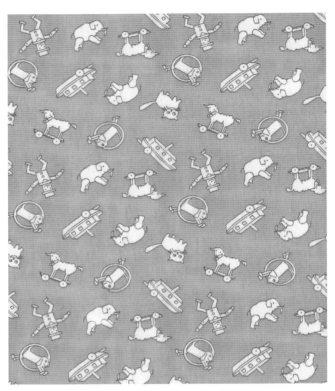

Pull toys and puppets.

Ducky's friends, 35" corduroy.

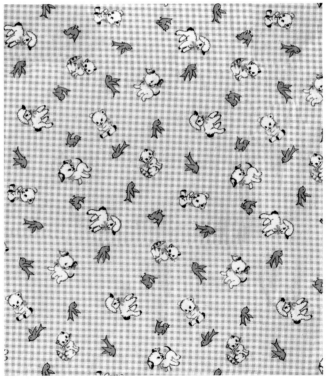

Lambs, kitty, and bear.

Leisure and Play

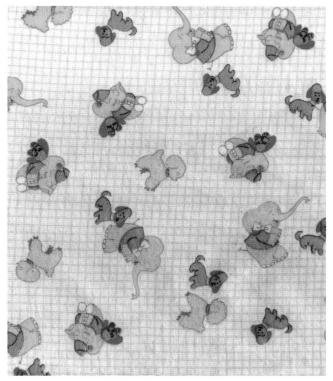

Baby takes a nap.

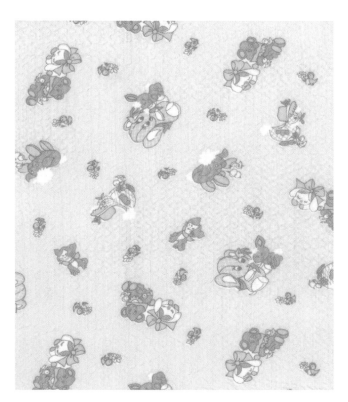

Washing up, 40" seersucker.

Humpty and pals, 34" light weight cotton.

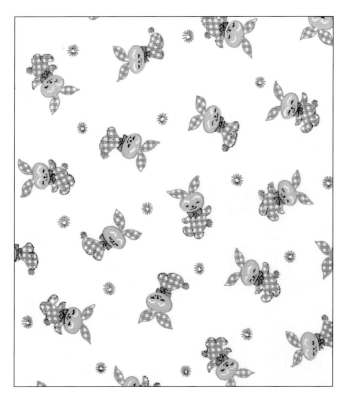

Stuffed bunnies in plaid, 36" percale with slight sheen.

Patches.

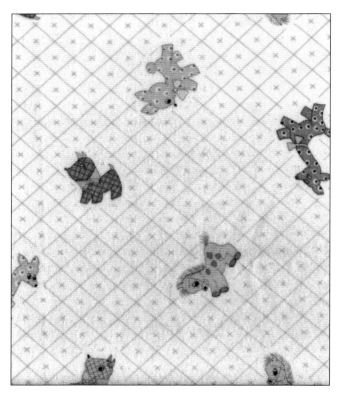

Stuffed giraffe and ponies.

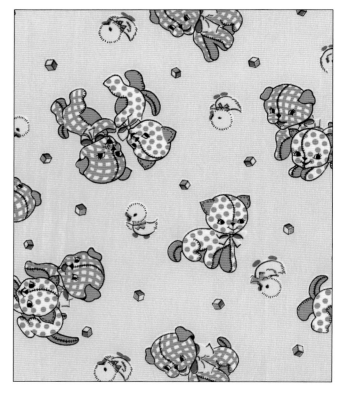

Gingham pup and polka dot cat, 35" tightly woven cotton.

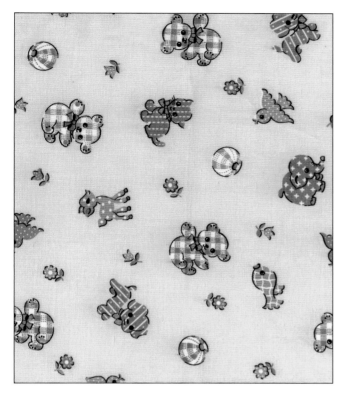

Stuffed babies.

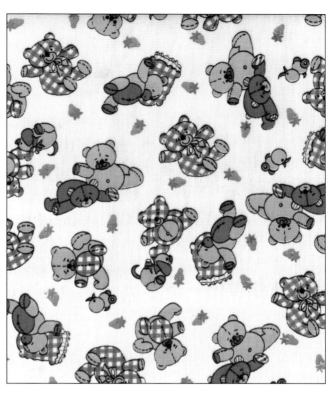

Stuffed bears, 32" coarsely woven cotton.

Stuffed buddies, 36" cotton with slight sheen.

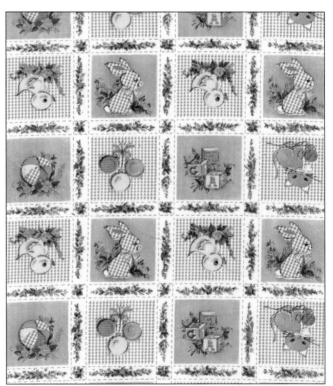

Stuffed bunnies, 35" percale.

Leisure and Play

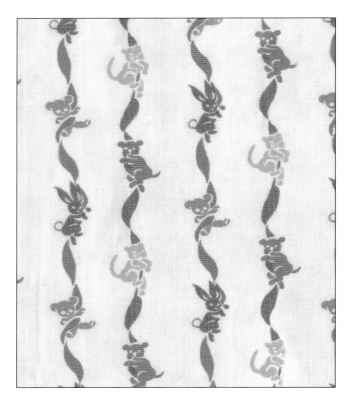 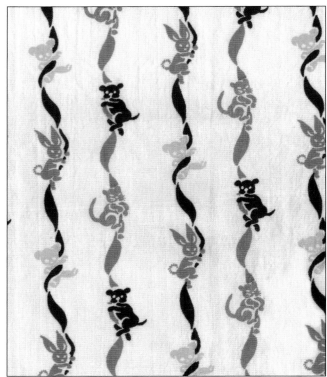

Ribbon play, feed sacks.

Appliqué babies.

Appliqué babies.

 Leisure and Play

Yarn dolls, feed sack.

Dressed in yellow bows.

Toucan and friends, 36" wide with possibly some rayon.

Chapter Four
Farm Life

This starts the chapter life on the farm. Many of them are, quite appropriately, feed sack material.

Included in this chapter is the "mouse meeting," as we had many of them on our farm. There didn't seem to be any snake fabric, for we had those as well. There were many fabrics of chicks, ducks, and geese, and I had difficulty distinguishing the difference between some of them, so please excuse any errors.

Farm life, 37" finely woven feed sack. This fabric was created in other color combinations (as are most of the fabrics), but I was unable to purchase a more colorful one.

Little house.

Fixing up, 36" brushed cotton.

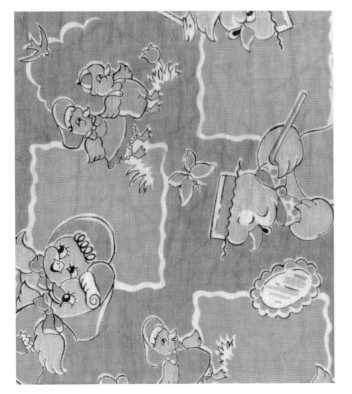

Chickie friends.

Chicken feed. This fabric was sewn into a child's smock. This is only a partial pattern.

Farm Life

Gathering the eggs.

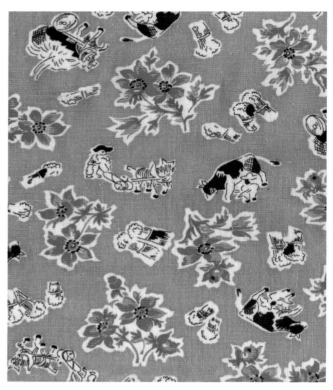

Working the farm, feed sack.

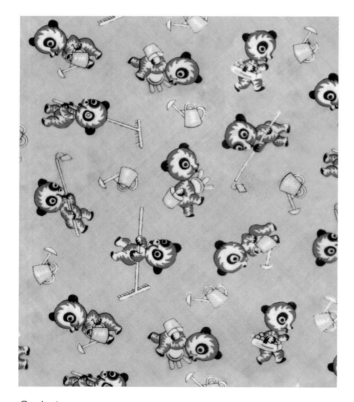

Gardening.

Pesky weeds… This fabric is unusual. I thought the fellow was a scout master, but decided he was a farmer. He first spots a pesky weed, reaches out to pull it, and lands on his seat. Believe me, I've done that a time or two in my garden!

Farm Life

In the orchard, 38" feed sack.

Vegetable people… This is 36" tightly woven fabric with crisp feel. I bet it was used as a tablecloth, as I'm not sure I'd want to wear it.

Fancy scarecrows, 35" cotton.

Scarecrows on duty, feed sack. I was especially anxious to purchase this fabric. I had used it in 1957 when attempting my first quilt, and still have that faded block.

Farm Life

Flower power, 35" cotton.

Picking flowers, 34" tightly woven cotton.

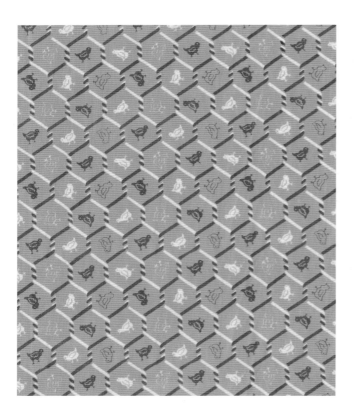

Chicken yard.

Caged chicks.

 Farm Life

Lambs in the flower garden, 36" coarsely woven cotton with additional texture thread.

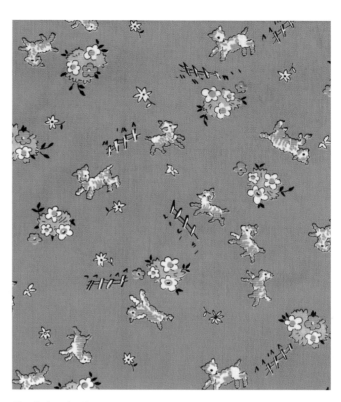

Gamboling lambs.

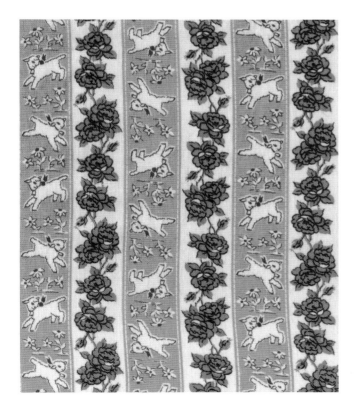

Catch me, feed sack.

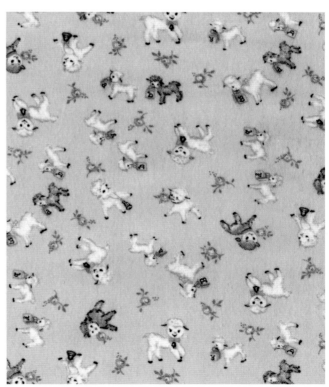

Lamb school, 36" rather stiff flannel.

Farm Life

In the field, 35" flannel.

Mouse meeting, percale quality.

Pony saddle, feed sack.

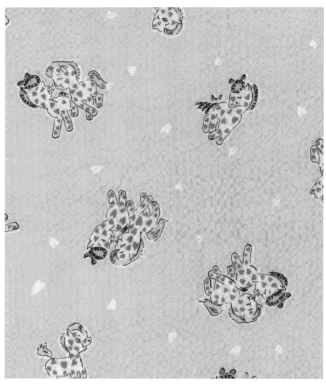

Pony pairs, 35" seersucker.

 Farm Life

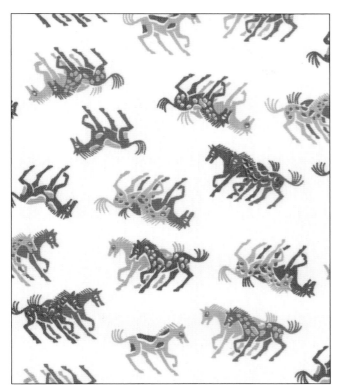

Prancing around, 36" feed sack like fabric.

Ponies, feed sack.

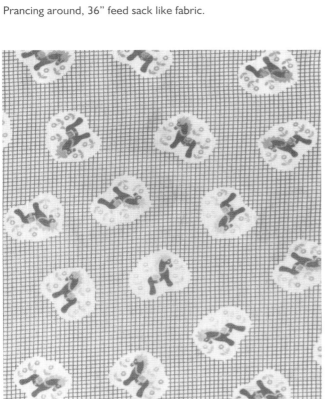

Through the barn door, 36" cotton.

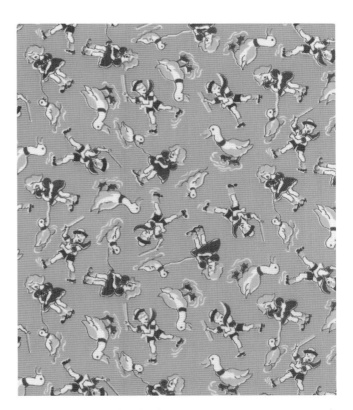

Guarding the geese, 36.5" tight weave crisp cotton.

Farm Life

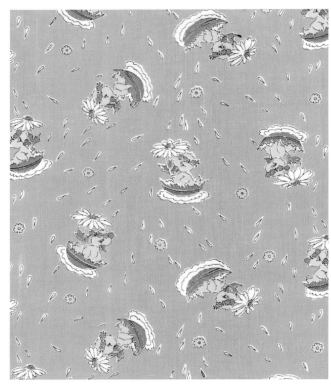

Ready for rain, percale quality. This is my favorite from this chapter — little ducks and their colorful umbrellas.

Splashing fun …

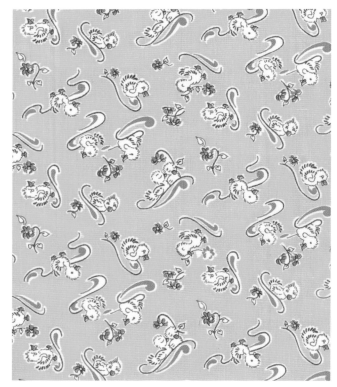

… in the puddle …

… and in the pond, 35.5" percale.

 Farm Life

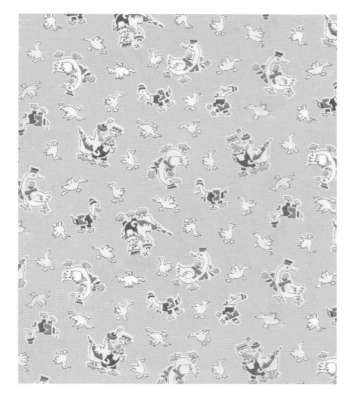

Mailman.

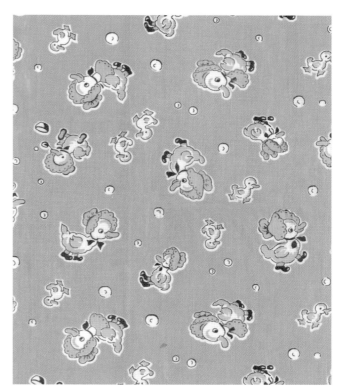

Baby bubbles.

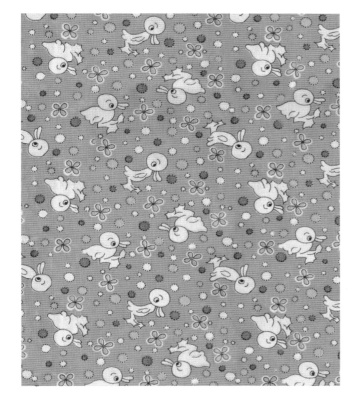

Looking for juicy worms.

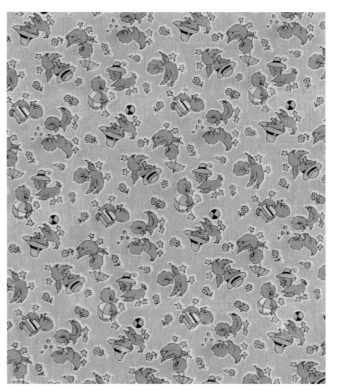

Time to party.

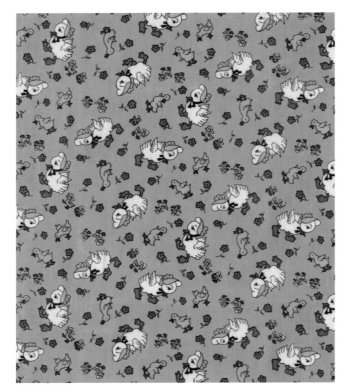

Wandering babies.

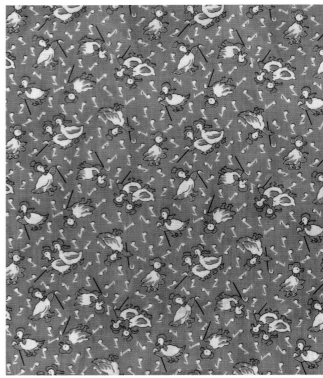

Out on the town.

Reunion day.

Quacker snack.

 Farm Life

Goose in top hat, in yellow and pink.

Bluebirds, 36" cotton.

Redbirds, 36" cotton.

Farm Life

Chapter Five
Kittens and Puppies

There are many joyful pets in the next images, but this first one, Kitty on Pink, seems especially appealing. Not all of the design is showing, but I tried to capture as much as possible. What little girl could resist it?

I enjoyed the fabric in "Mama's Watching," as it clearly shows that Mama has her eye on that little one.

President Roosevelt's Scottie dog was very popular during his presidency. This is reflected in the wide variety of "Scottie" dog fabrics available at the time.

Kitty on pink, 35" lightweight cotton, almost gauzelike.

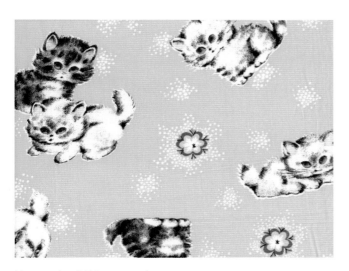

Kitty so shy, 36" heavyweight cotton.

Kittens on yellow, 35" cotton.

Kitty pranks, 36" cotton.

Nickel soda. This fabric has an endearing theme — the character has a nickel to spend, searches the candy counter, but spends it on his lady friend.

Kitty litter. This was a badly soiled piece of quilt backing, but after much soaking cleaned enough to use.

Kitties on orange, 35.5" cotton.

Green-eyed kitties, 35" cotton.

Kitty on parade.

The themes in these photos are similar – I hope you can see the clever kittens hiding in the cotton patch.

In the willow bush, 36" feed sack.

In the cotton patch, 35.5" heavyweight flannel.

Blue kitty, red kitty.

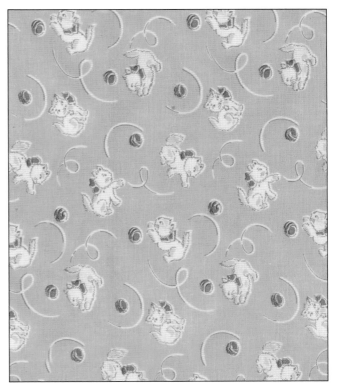

Playing ball.

Kittens and Puppies

Kitty and butterflies.

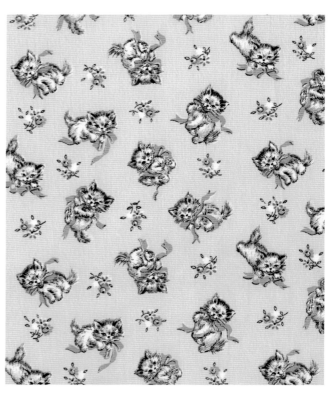

Kitty with pink bow, 35.5" tightly woven cotton. Isn't this smiling kitty hard to resist?

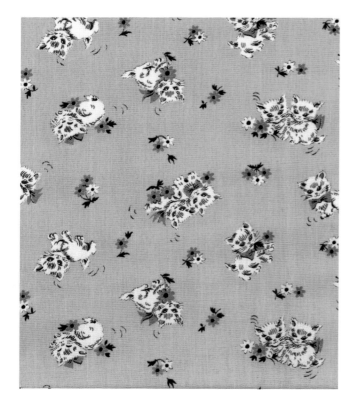

In the daisy garden.

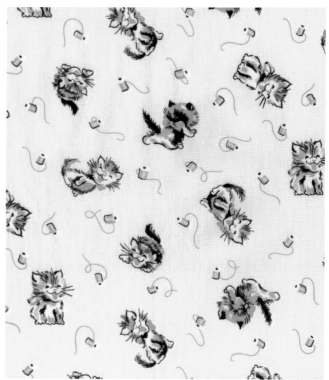

Laughing kitty, 35" cotton.

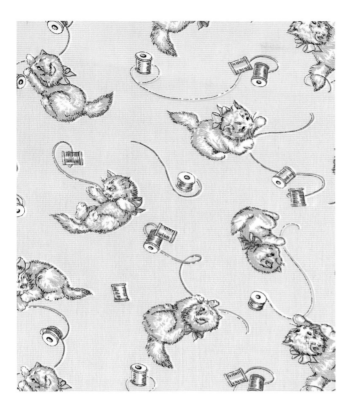

Helping Mama, 36" percale.

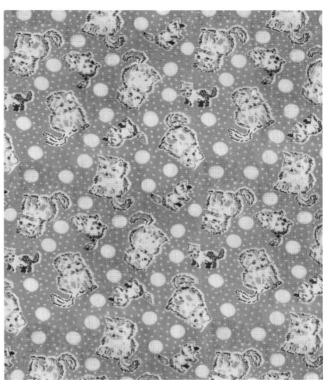

Mama's watching.

Rich kitty, poor kitty… There may be a nursery rhyme here. I first thought of city mouse and country mouse, but don't know of a version for cats. Obviously, the rich kitty is attracted to the poor kitty. Don't know his plan!

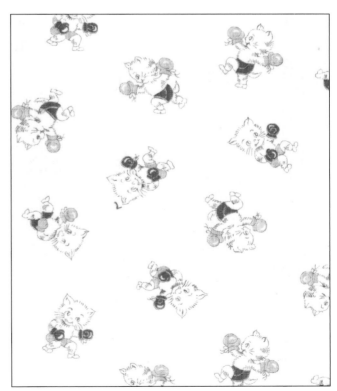

Kitty boxer, 32" seersucker.

Kittens and Puppies

Meow, meow.

Kitty cluster, 36" large blister seersucker.

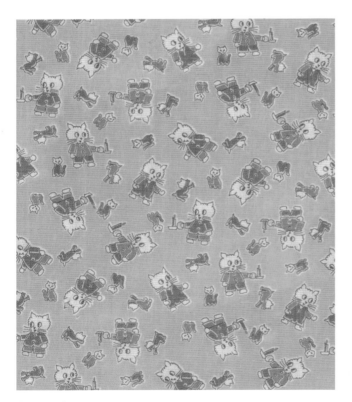

Lighting the way.

Kitty bow.

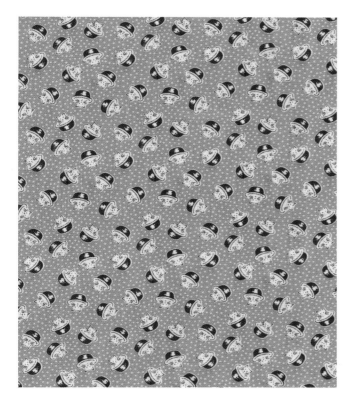

Kitty in the bowl.

Kitty, gold fabric.

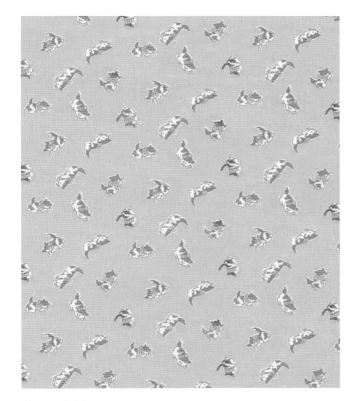

Kitty, pink fabric.

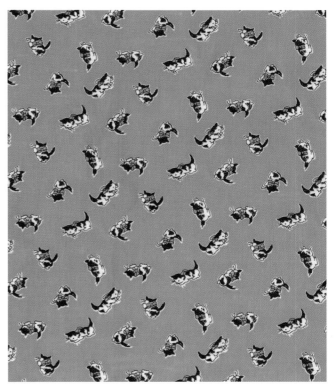

Kitty, turquoise fabric.

Kittens and Puppies

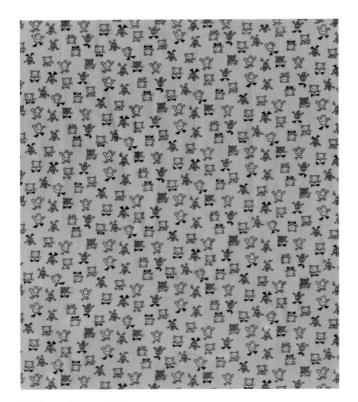

Kitties and pups, 38" cotton.

Puppies and kitties, 36" cotton with crisp feel.

Puppies and kitties.

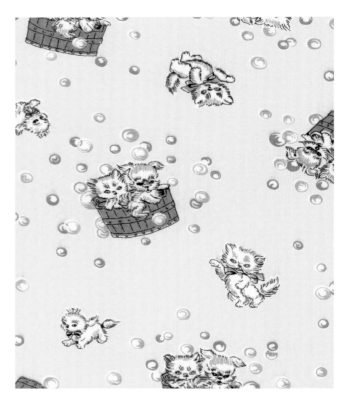

In the wash tub.

 Kittens and Puppies

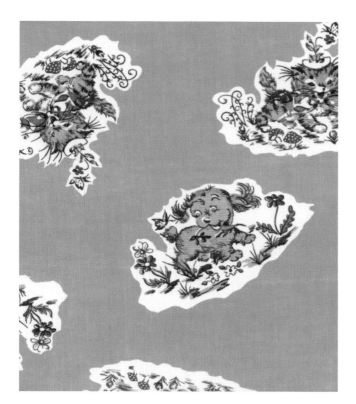

In the flower patch, 35" cotton, in blue and yellow.

Playful collies, 35" high quality cotton with slight sheen.

Foxy Parisian.

French poodles in Paris, 36" percale quality.

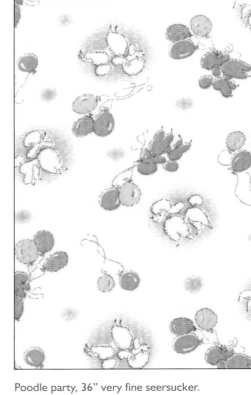

Poodle party, 36" very fine seersucker.

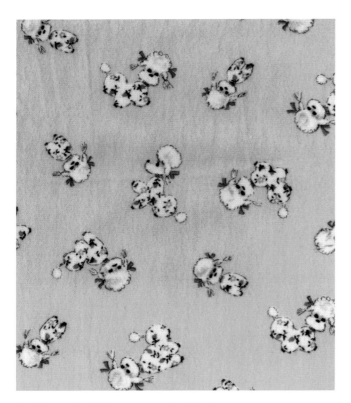

Poodle petals, 35" loose weave brushed cotton.

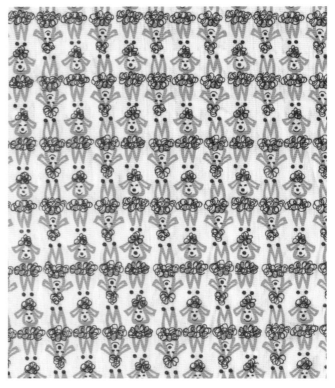

Poodle pups.

Pups on grid, 36" cotton.

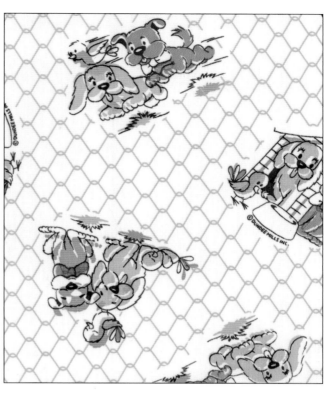

Doghouse pals, 37" cotton.

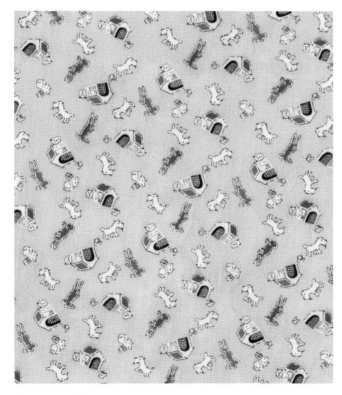

Doghouse visitor.

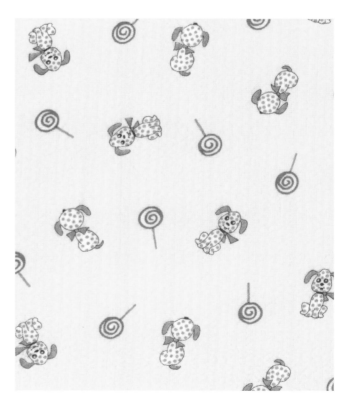

Spot and lollipops, 36" seersucker.

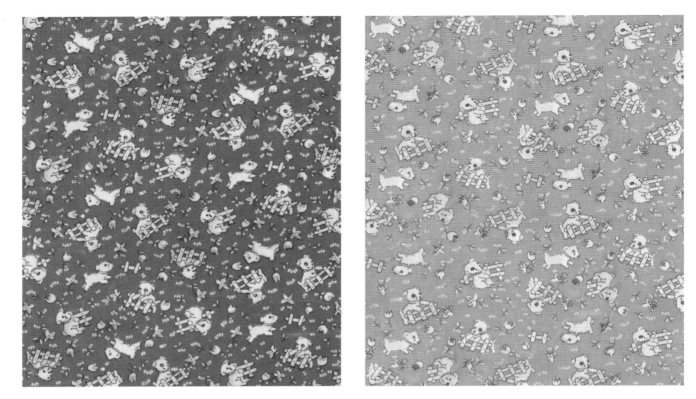

That fence can't hold me, red and pink fabric.

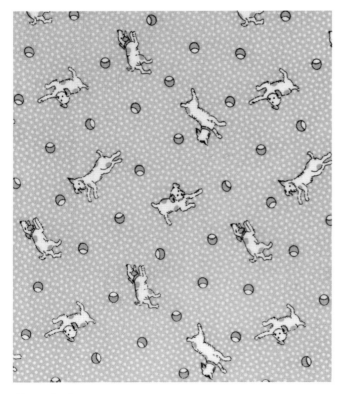

Playing fetch.

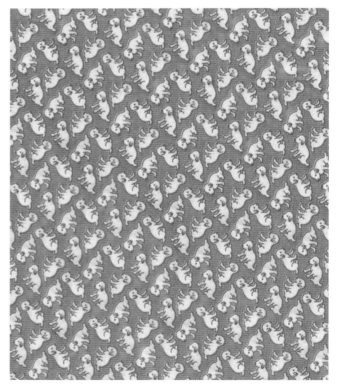

Pups on red.

 Kittens and Puppies

Pups on pink.

Pups on blue.

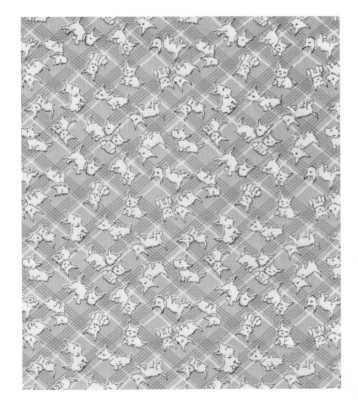

Scotties on plaid.

Tartan Scotties.

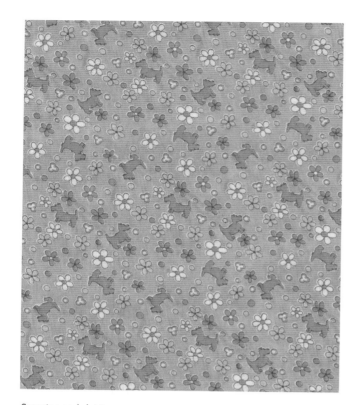

Scotties and daisies.

Scottie ribbons

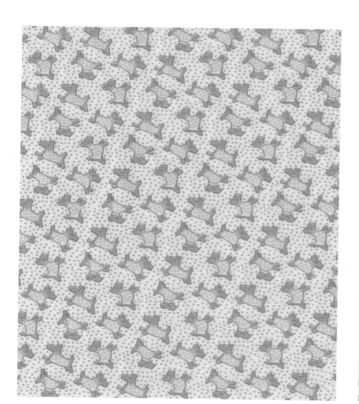

Pink Scotties.

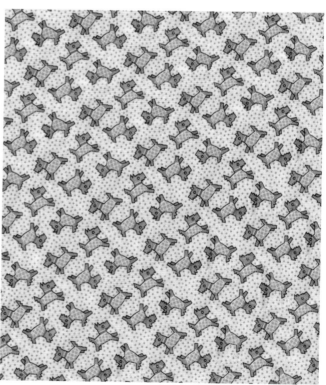

Blue Scotties.

 Kittens and Puppies

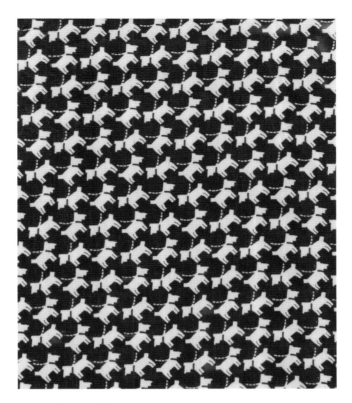

Scotties, brown fabric.

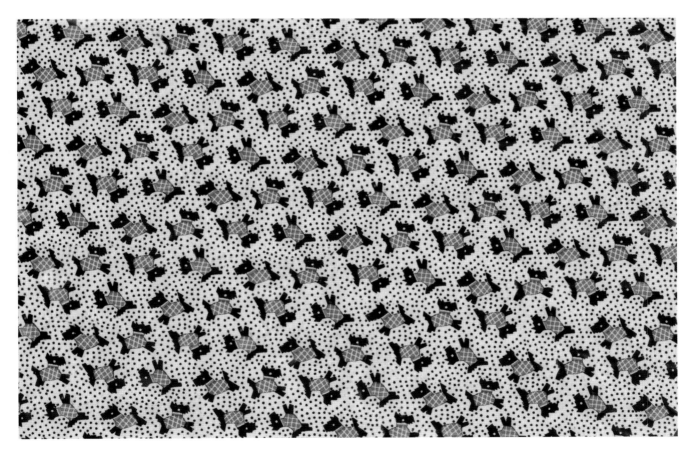

Black Scotties.

Kittens and Puppies

Chapter Six
Forest and Jungle

The fabrics in this chapter contain images of wild animals (as opposed to the domestic animals in Chapter Four). There are lots of bunnies and bears, and even penguins and pandas.

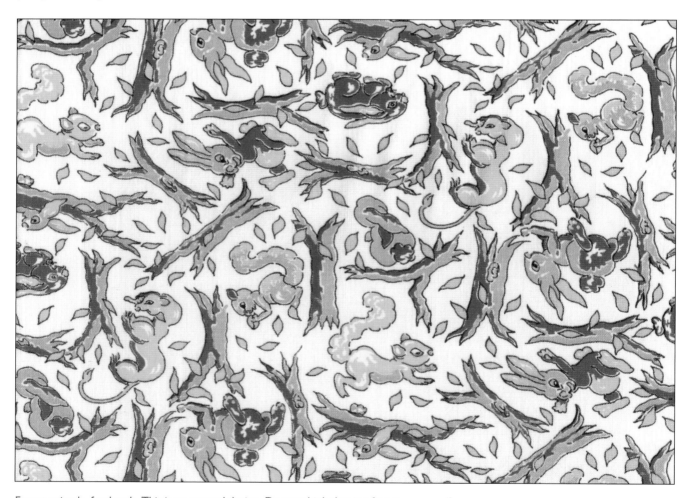

Forest animals, feed sack. This is an unusual design. Do you think that is a ferret or weasel?

Deer pals, 35.5" cotton with two reds in background.

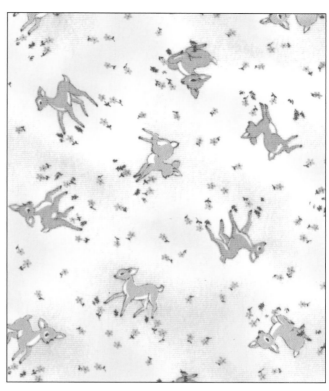

Dear little deer, 36" medium weight flannel.

Leaping Impala, 36" feed sack.

Jungle secrets, 36" tightly woven cotton. This fabric looks like the animal prints so popular the last few years, but it has been in my possession for quite some time.

Forest and Jungle

Courting bears on blue.

Courting bears on red.

Beary love, 35" seersucker.

Singing bears, 35.5" medium weight cotton.

 Forest and Jungle

Skiers training. This fabric is from a vintage Dresden plate block. The three small pieces were just enough to contain the repeats.

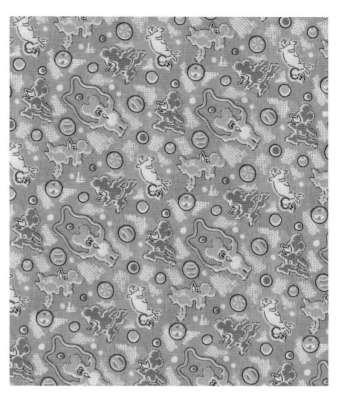

Jump rope and racing. This image is also comprised of three small squares with just enough fabric to clone.

Jump rope contest, 36" corduroy.

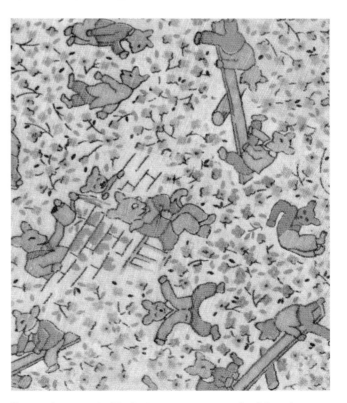

Beary joke, swatch. Much time was spent on this fabric, but not all of the design was available. This is an enlarged swatch of fabric with as much design as I could get in one piece. See the water being poured on Grandpa and the youngster laughing?

Forest and Jungle

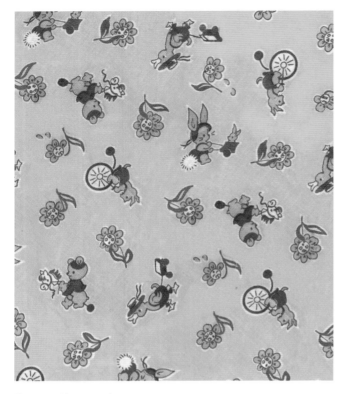

Bears and bunny rides.

Bunnies, bears, and blocks. This fabric is from a child's bib.

It's this big.

Balloons and carrots.

 Forest and Jungle

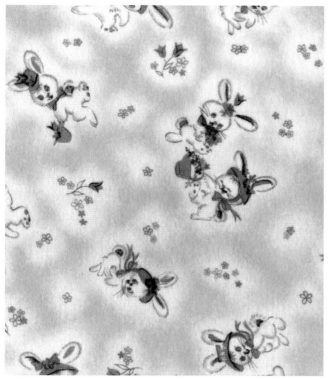

Picking posies, 35.5" flannel.

Bunny grins, 37" feed sack.

So shy.

Peace dove.

Probably the most time spent on any fabric was in these images. The fabric was taped and scanned several times, but each time the cloning process showed the work was incorrect. When it was finally finished (six months later), I found there were fifteen different characters in the design.

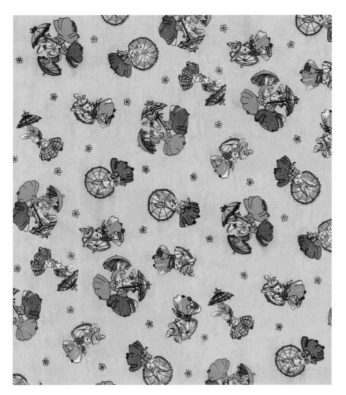 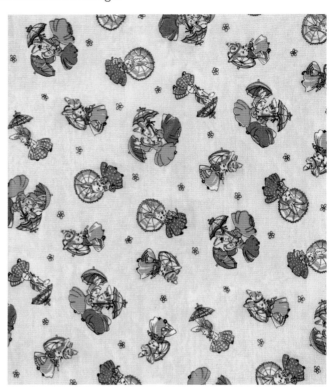

Parasol pals, both 36" cotton.

 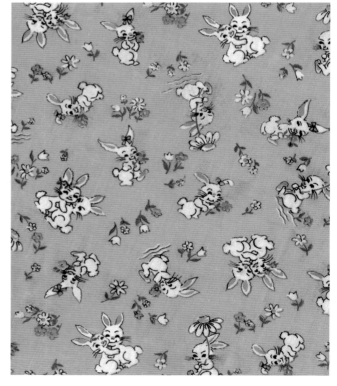

Daisy umbrella.

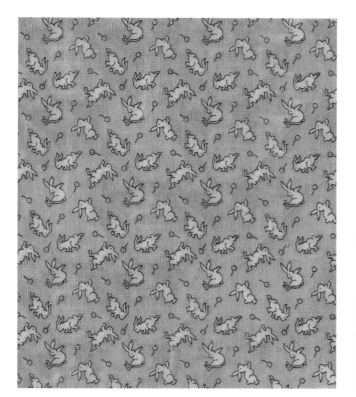

The bunny hop.

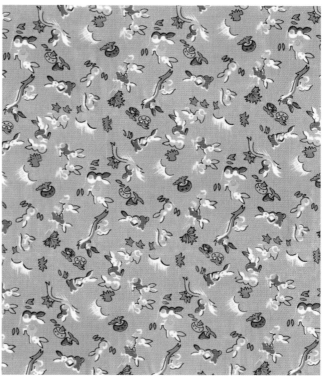

Bunny snack, percale quality.

Bunny and roses, 36" feed sack.

So blue, feed sack.

Forest and Jungle

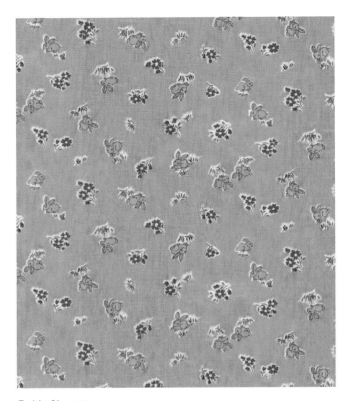

Field of bunnies.

All the grandkids.

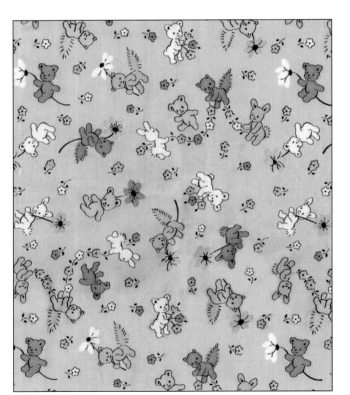

Bushy tail, 35" cotton, on blue and white.

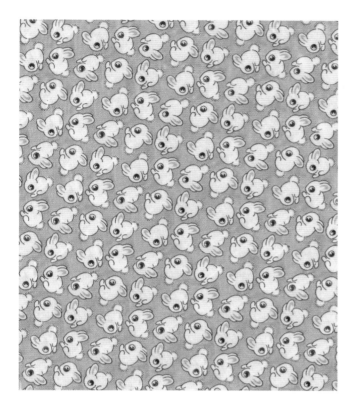

Bright-eyed bunny, 35" tightly woven cotton.

Ghost animals.

Panda play.

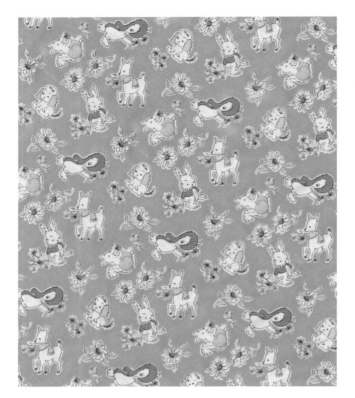

In from the cold.

Penguin and pals.

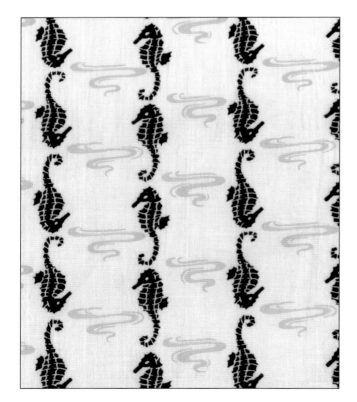

Seahorse splashes, feed sack.

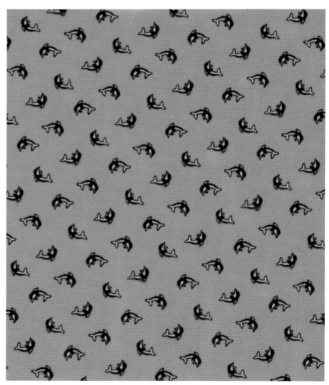

Jumping fish.

Forest and Jungle

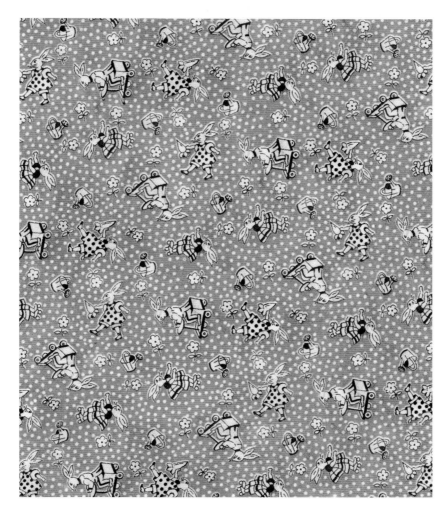

Moving along… This was the second fabric in my grandmother's quilt top. I'm so glad those quilt tops were not finished, as these two fabrics are special to me.

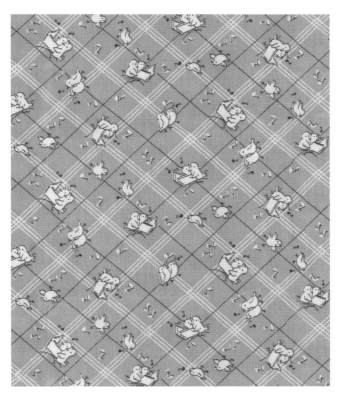

Songbird tweeters, 4" quilt blocks.

Forest and Jungle

Chapter Seven
Trains, Planes, and Automobiles

There were a few fabrics with designs of cars, trains, and other forms of transportation, so I combined the various modes of moving from one place to another. It's interesting that walking doesn't show up! Anyway, what child doesn't think of floating around in the sky? (I dreamed of flying many times as a child. What a disappointment when I woke.) Ballooning would be one way of flying and the various images show us how.

The number of ship fabrics surprised me, although we may have been more conscious of them during and after World War II.

We finally come to the more recent years with space travel. Although the four fabrics here are very nice, the best feed sack in this theme I've seen sold on eBay in excess of $165. Needless to say, it sold to someone else. Don't we always want the one that got away?

Ballooning, 34.5" tightly woven cotton.

Scouting around, 35" medium weight cotton.

Sky full. This fabric is from an apron.

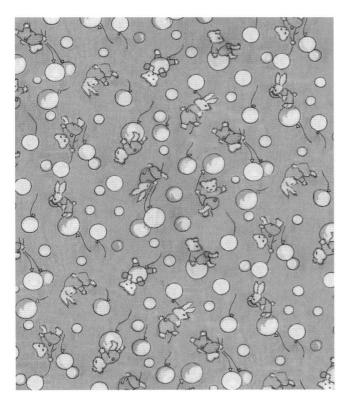

Can you see it yet?

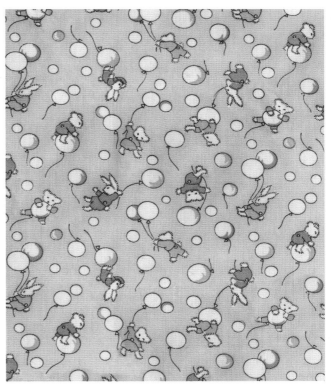

Up, up, and away…

Trains, Planes, and Automobiles

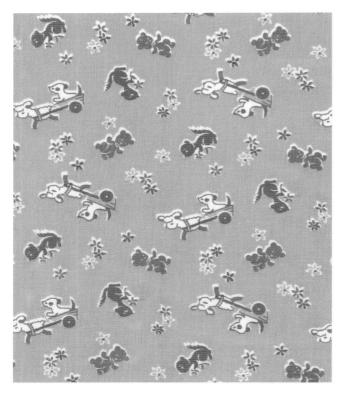

Gitty up, feed sack.

Bunny ride, 35" feed sack.

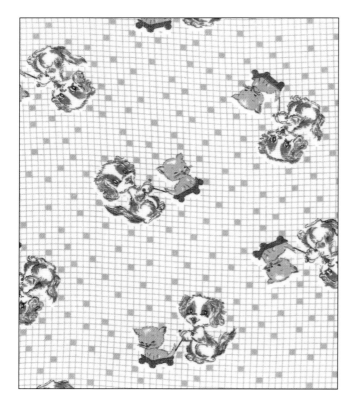

Kitty in the wagon.

Swan cart, 36" feed sack.

Trains, Planes, and Automobiles

The Egyptian design in these photos was very old fabric in a vintage quilt top,
but the complete design was available, so I've included them here.

Camel ride.

Elephant ride.

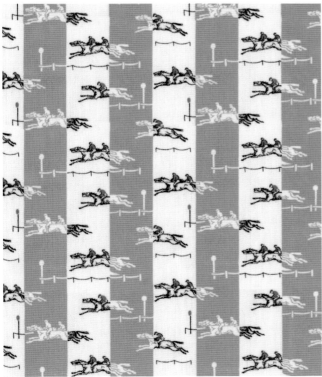

Horse racing.

Unusual trike.

Scooter race, feed sack, white. One is blue themed; the other red.

Scooter race, feed sack.

Scooters and wagons. This one is from quilt scraps sold as vintage fabric. It seems so bright and colorful that I'm not convinced it is indeed old. Perhaps you, one of the readers, will know.

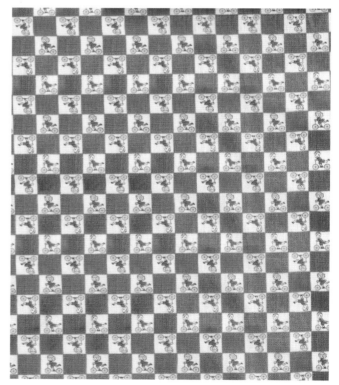

Scooter ride.

Jelly bean man, 38" cotton plisse.

Firefighters.

Firemen, 34" flannel.

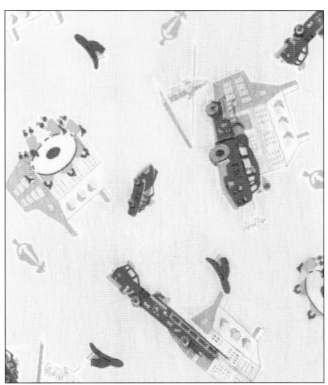

Firehouse. This is another piece from that very stained quilt backing I mentioned in Chapter Five. It was soaked and washed several times and, although an incomplete design, finally usable.

Sailboat patches.

Sailboat races.

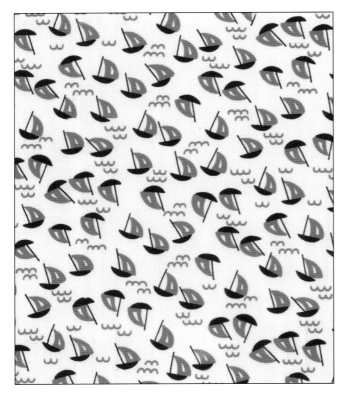

Sailboats.

Sailing around.

Yachting.

Sunday sail, 36" feed sack.

Sailing ships and flags, 34" cotton.

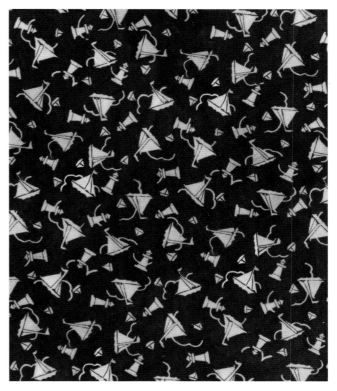

Sailing ships and buoys.

Train play. This fabric is from a little boy's romper. The design was large and only part of it is included here.

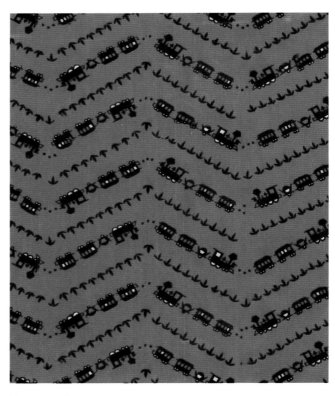

Trains at night.

Trains and planes, 36" feed sack.

Now, how does this work? 36" feed sack.

Trains, Planes, and Automobiles

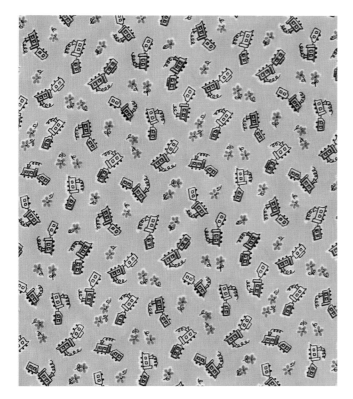

Wee trains.

Early engines, 35" cotton.

Riding along.

Spiffy prancer.

Vintage automobile.

Early racers, 36" feed sack.

Rockets in space.

Space explorers, 35.5" textured cotton blend.

Space ride, 36" seersucker.

Space travel, 37.5" light weight cotton.

Trains, Planes, and Automobiles

Chapter Eight
Wild West and Miscellaneous

Today's children are probably not as conscious of the early west as children of a few years ago. I was pleased to find the fabric of George Washington.

I expect that some of the Western themed fabrics decorated many a little boy's room, excepting the Indian maiden fabric, of course. I noticed they were in mostly in reds and blues. There was a period that red, white, and blue was a popular combination for children's rooms. I, too, used that as a decorating theme many years ago.

There were some fabrics that just didn't seem to go anywhere in particular, so they were grouped under miscellaneous, depicting lifestyles in various parts of the country and different kinds of apparel.

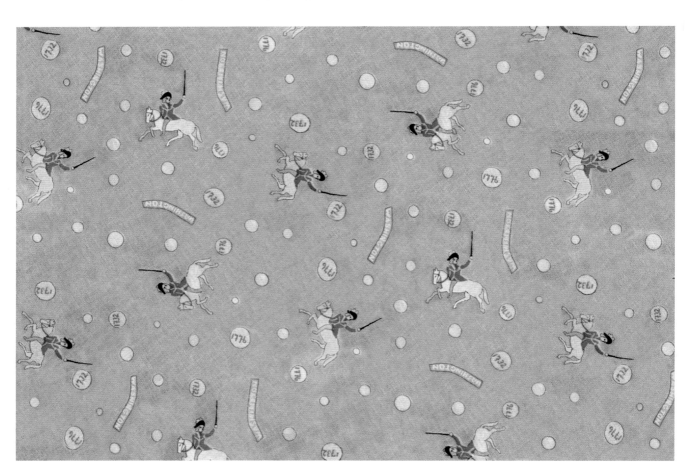

George Washington in Battle. This fabric is from a disintegrating quilt top; however, these pieces were usable, and I was able to clone a complete design. Here's a lesson for a child — he was born in 1732, and independence was declared in 1776.

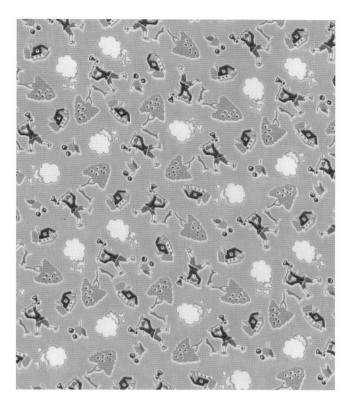

George Washington and the cherry tree.

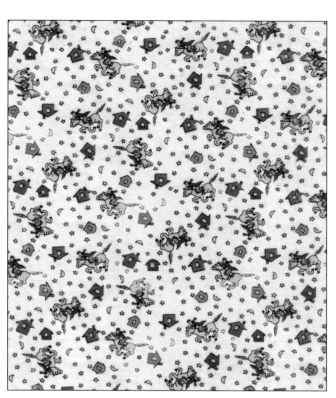

Paul Revere's ride.

Soldiers in basic training, feed sack. When I purchased this fabric, I thought it was the same fabric as the "Soldiers' March" swatch, but not so. I don't know what kind of a gun it is that knocks the "soldier" over. Doesn't look like anything I recognize.

Soldiers march, swatch. This fabric is from an old quilt purchased in Paducah. Parts of the design are missing, but an enlarged swatch was included since the themes are similar.

Wild West and Miscellaneous

Hup, one, two, 36" percale.

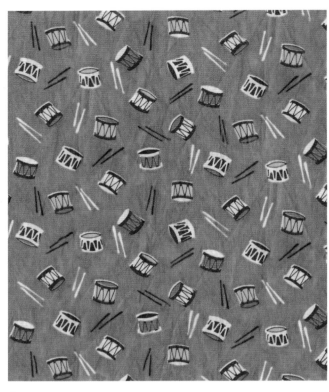

Colonial drums.

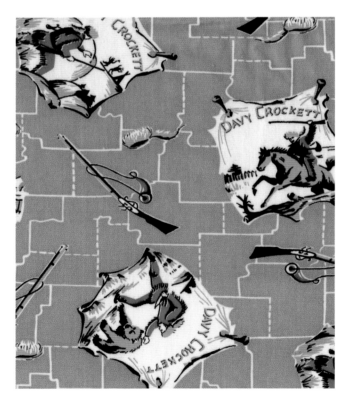

Davy Crockett, 35" cotton.

Davy and the bear, 37" loosely woven cotton.

Daniel Boone's cabin, 37" feed sack.

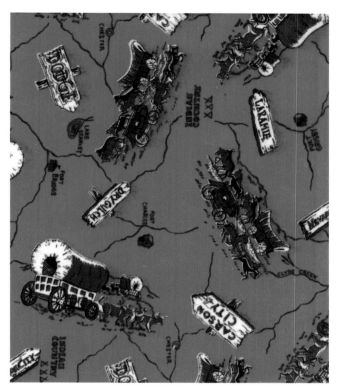

Westward ho.

Western train, 36" cotton.

Indian target.

Indian camp, 36" denim-like cotton.

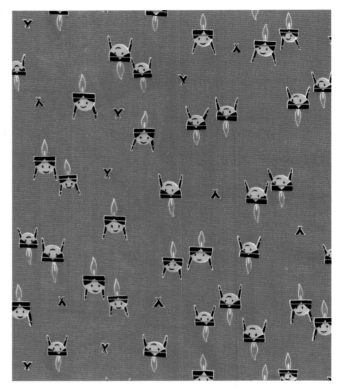

Indian maiden.

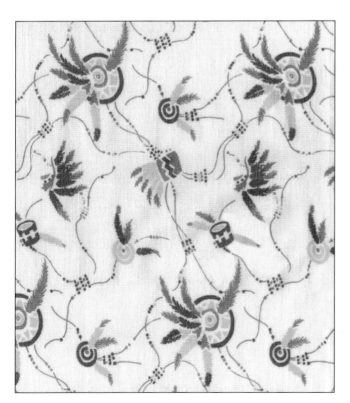

Indian headdress, feed sack.

Frontiersmen and Indians, 36" medium weight flannel.

Ridin' and ropin', 36" crisp cotton.

Riding the range.

Branding time, 35" cotton.

Bucking bronco.

Rodeo practice.

Rodeo day.

Western heroes, 37.5" cotton.

Playing Indians, 30" seersucker.

Cowgirls and cowboys, 35" cotton.

Wild ride.

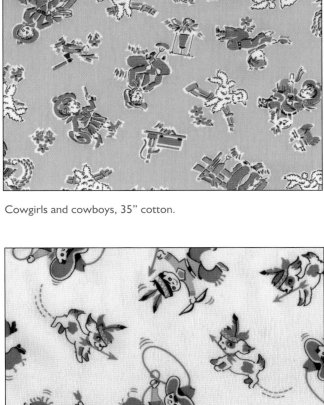

Ropin' man, 35" lightly textured cotton, probably pajama fabric.

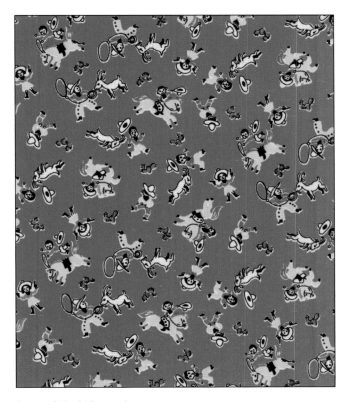

Roping Billy, 36" percale.

Wild West and Miscellaneous

Little cowboy.

Whoopee.

Ride 'em cowboy.

Colonial life, 36" feed sack.

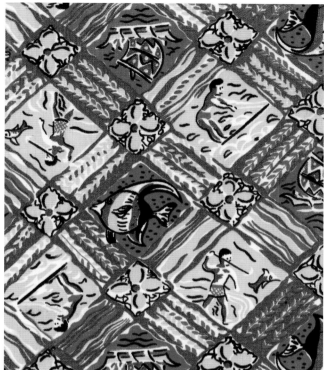

Hawaiian life 1.

Hawaiian life 2.

Indian life, 35" finely woven cotton.

Mexican life.

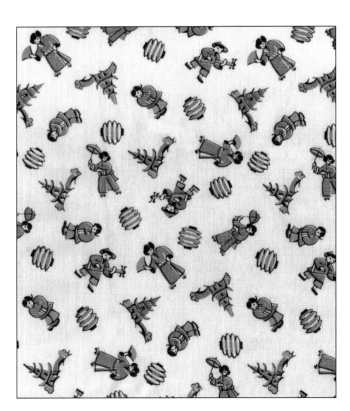
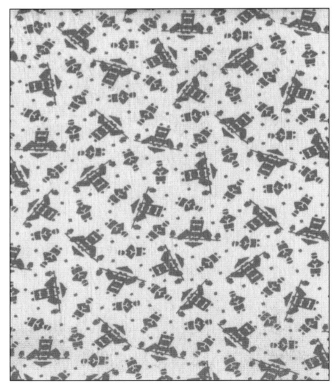

Asian life and Asian lanterns, 37" feed sacks.

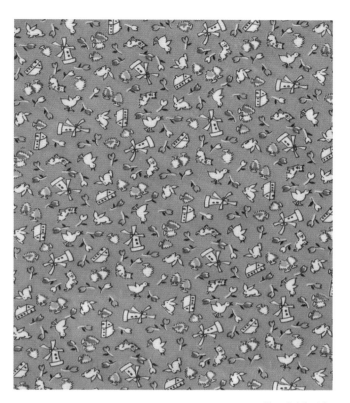
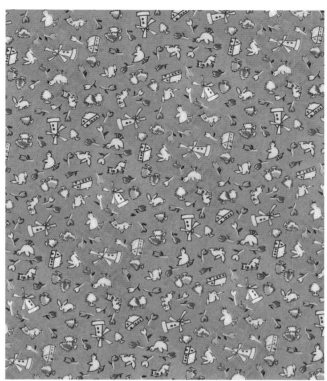

Dutch life, blue and purple fabric.

Windmills, Dutch shoes, and tulips.

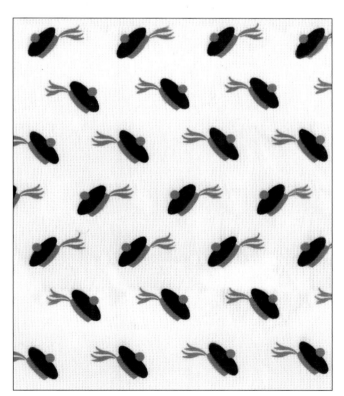

Tams.

Bows on blue, 36" feed sack.

Bows on pink, 36" feed sack.

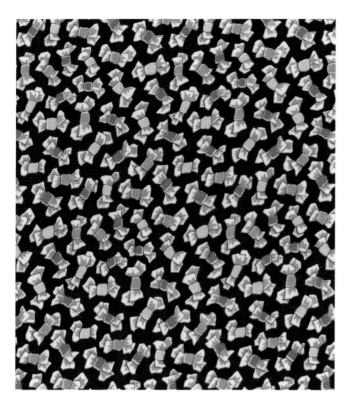

Tiny bows, feed sack.

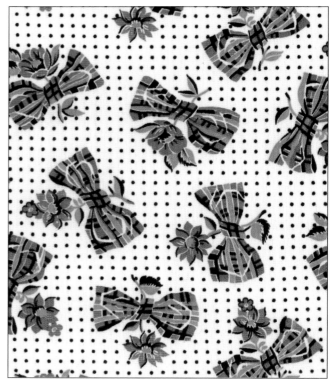

Bows in plaid, 36" light weight cotton.

Party parasols, feed sack.

Raindrops keep falling, feed sack.

Baby shoes.

Deliveries.

Moon fishing, 36" seersucker.

Moon ride.

Mermaid school, 34.5" cotton. This especially sweet fabric shows mermaids reading, sewing, and cutting paper dolls.

Flower fairies, feed sack.

Elf babies. This wonderful fabric was a child's bonnet. The designer had a terrific imagination.

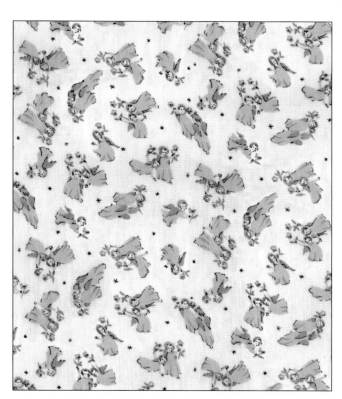

Angels. This tiny design is from a 3-inch doll skirt. The angels look just like angels should.

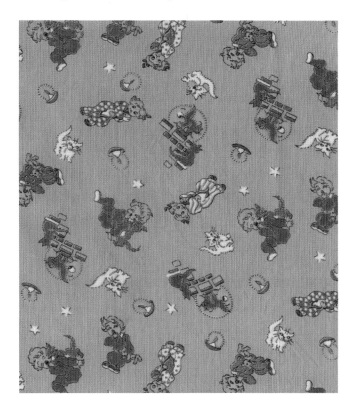

Nodding off. This fabric came from Australia. It seemed appropriate to end the chapter with a little nap.

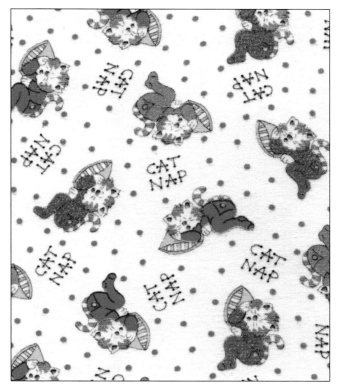

Catnap.

Good night baby.

Now I lay me down to sleep, 35" cotton.

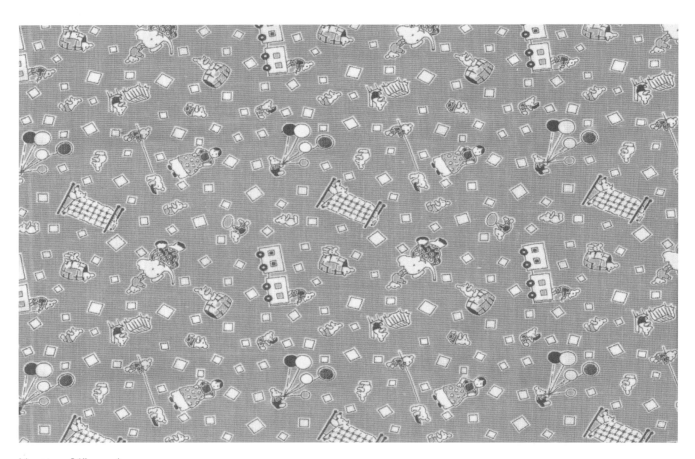

Nap time, 36" percale.

 *Wild West and Miscellaneous*

Chapter Nine
Swatches

Many of the fabrics discovered were only small pieces or incomplete designs. Trying to decide how to present them, I overlaid pieces with similar themes and scanned them. This seemed to work so the next twenty-five images in this chapter are swatches of over 125 different fabrics. One contains my original Mary's lamb fabric. There are also a swatch of Jack and Jill, where Jack gets a spanking. Not nice, after he broke his crown!

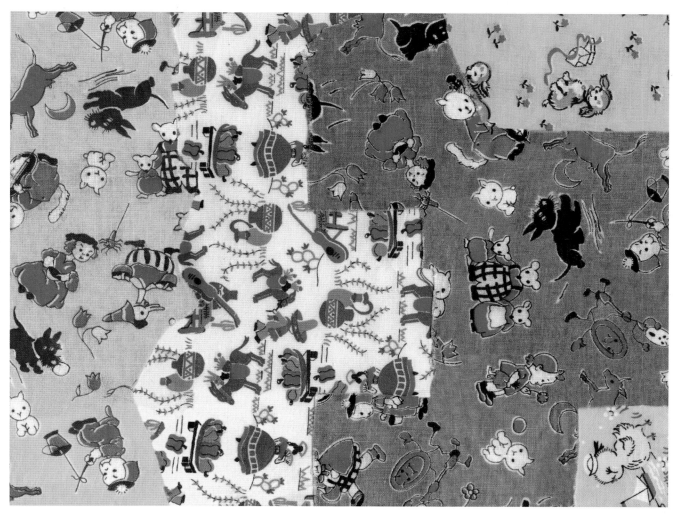

Nursery rhymes. Notice the two colors of wonderful fabric. There is "Little Miss Muffet," "Mother Goose," "Three Blind Mice," and "The Cat and The Fiddle." I'm not sure why the little fellow is fishing in a bucket, but there probably is a reason. I believe this designer is the same as in the "Elf Babies" fabric found in the previous chapter.

Babies.

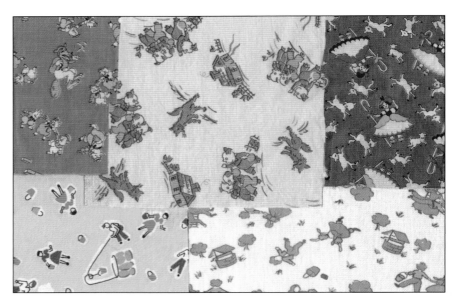

Nursery rhymes.

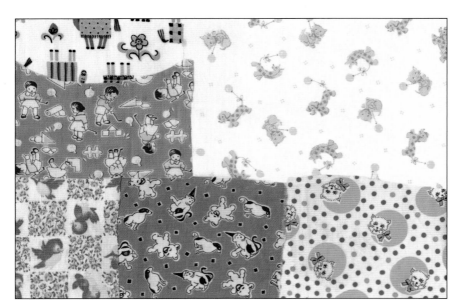

Playtime.

 Swatches

130

Circus.

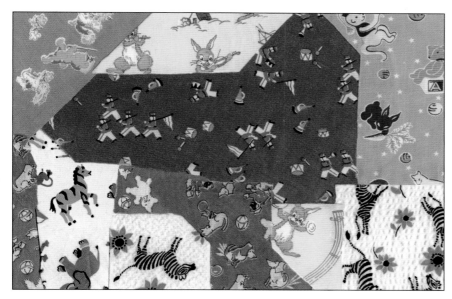

Circus and bands.

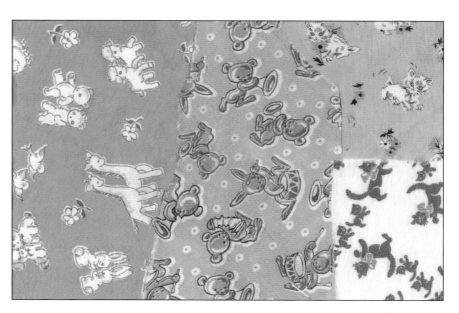

Bunny band.

Swatches

Activities.

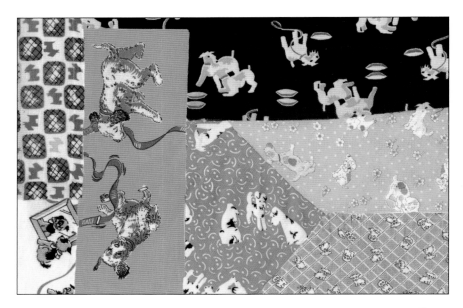

Pups.

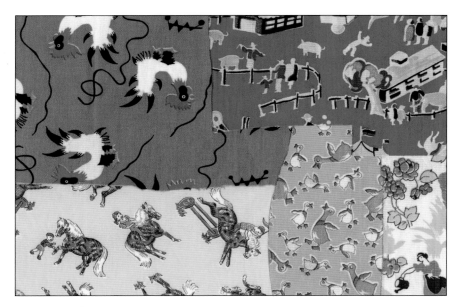

Farm life.

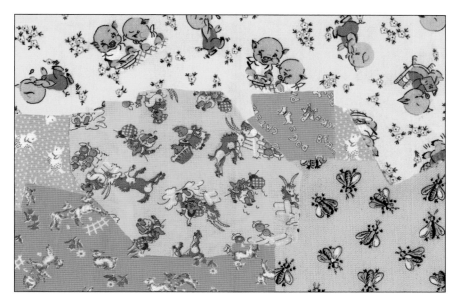

Goats, pigs, and lambs. This image has a fabric of note in the center. You can see Mr. Billy Goat pushing the youngster over the fence where he falls in a puddle. I'll bet that youngster irritated him one too many times! Mama puts him in the washtub and then hangs him up to dry.

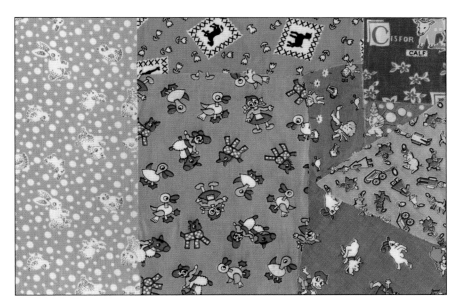

Blue boys.

Bunnies and birds.

Water babies.

Travel.

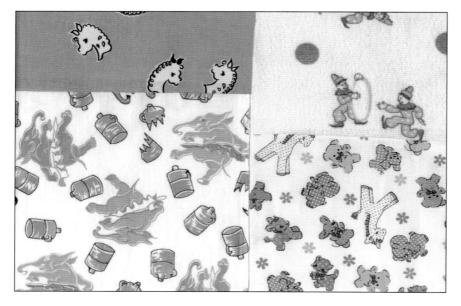

Demon rum. This fabric contains an unusual theme. At the bottom left it appears to be a demon snarling with broken jugs around. Would demon rum be a fabric you would wear? Well, perhaps my imagination has gone too far.

Guy stuff.

More stuff.

Indian games.

Swatches

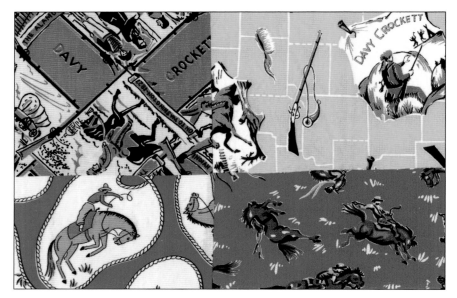

Cowboys 1.

Cowboys 2.

Cowboys 3.

 Swatches

Cowboys 4.

Cowboys 5.

Cowboys 6.

Swatches

Chapter Ten

These fabrics were too large to scan and so they were photographed to finish the collection. I believe most of them were used for children's furnishings perhaps curtains, pillows, tablecloths, or bedspreads.

Escaping Bo Peep, fine percale.

Tummy ache – too many carrots, 35" percale.

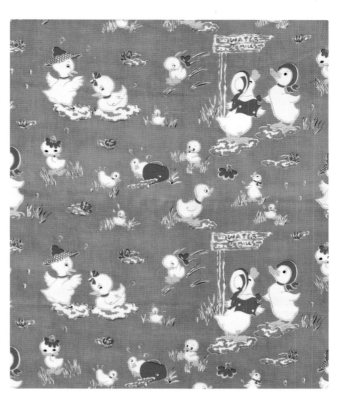

Two miles to the lake, 35" lightweight cotton.

Fairy Princess and her subjects, 34" percale.

Watering the flowers, 34" feed sack.

Large Print Fabrics

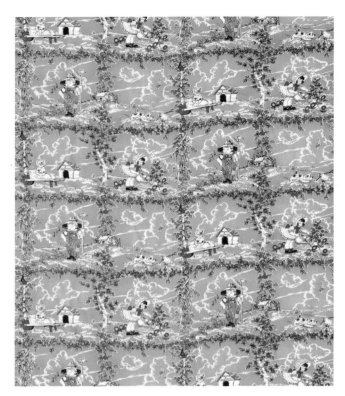

Dad, Mom, Patches, and Whiskers, 36" feed sack. I've also seen this fabric in various pinks and beige.

Farm chores, 34" cotton.

The circus is in town, 35" soft cotton with slight sheen.

Here come the clowns, 35.5" lightweight cotton.

Three-ring circus, 35.5" cotton.

Band rehearsal, 37" lightweight cotton.

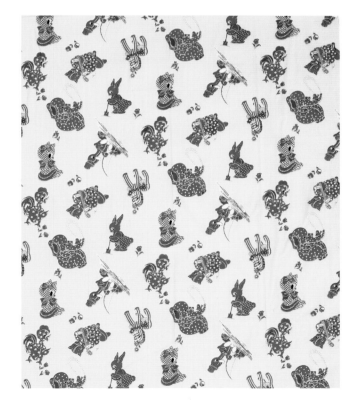

Calico pals, 35" medium weight cotton.

Hey Mama, what's this? 38" feed sack.

Blue-eyed kitty, 35.5" percale.

Puppy tricks, 35" lightweight cotton.

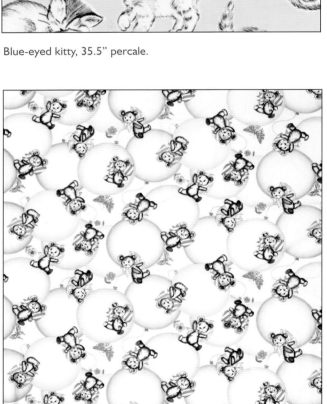

Butterflies, balloons, and bears, 35" percale.

Barnyard friends, 35" percale.

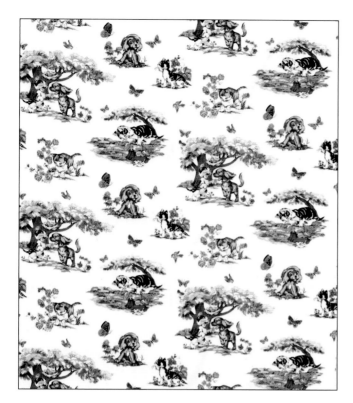

Hide and Seek, measurement unknown.

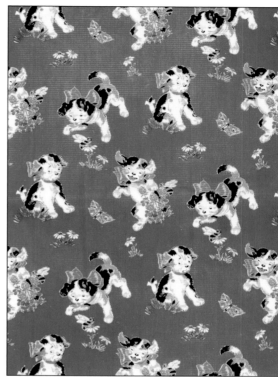

Butterflies, bees, and puppies, 34.5" percale.

Wishing on a Star, 35" lightweight cotton.

Native Costumes, 35" feed sack.

Water, water... Water everywhere, 34" chintz.